How to Make

Money

Homesteading

Self Sufficient and

Happy Life

Charles Milne

versions of the work, both physical, digital, and audio unless express consent of the Publisher is provided beforehand. Any additional rights reserved.

Furthermore, the information that can be found within the pages described forthwith shall be considered both accurate and truthful when it comes to the recounting of facts. As such, any use, correct or incorrect, of the provided information will render the Publisher free of responsibility as to the actions taken outside of their direct purview. Regardless, there are zero scenarios where the original author or the Publisher can be deemed liable in any fashion for any damages or hardships that may result from any of the information discussed herein.

Additionally, the information in the following pages is intended only for informational purposes and should thus be thought of as universal. As befitting its nature, it is presented without assurance regarding its prolonged validity or interim quality. Trademarks that are mentioned are done without written consent and can in no way be considered an endorsement from the trademark holder.

Introductions

Modern housekeeping is a perfect way to save some of your hard-earned money. That's if you're not afraid of a bit of hard work and getting up before the rooster. Today's fast-paced world of luxury will and does drive you down the road to debt. Homesteading comes from the Homestead Act of 1862. Settlers from all walks of life, single mothers, slaves and immigrants fresh off the sea, took up the gauntlet for five years to build a house and live peacefully on 160 acres. They had been tasked with making changes and "holding the ground" over the five-year period. Two witnesses, friends or neighbors, then, through their signature, vouched for the hard work. The homesteader would also obtain a grant from the President of the United States. Now, homesteading is still alive and well, but there is not any free land to be granted. However, those who are homesteading today are trying to imitate the main characteristics of those early homesteaders, their self-reliance, and tenacity. Today's homesteading can be accomplished on any piece of land, no matter how big or small, and is still very much about self-reliance.

Early homesteaders, by necessity, lived a strong existence. They didn't have strength, no drinking water; they were forced to hunt, cook their own meat, and produce their own crops. They were expected to find ways to maintain their food from one harvest to the next, and even longer if crops were killed by nature or other unexpected incidents. For many peppers homesteading is a logical choice.

Modern homesteading focuses on reducing carbon consumption, minimizing waste, and cultivating or pursuing your own food by choice. People today want to lead this self-reliant, easier, but certainly, hard-working lifestyle because they enjoy the independence and prosperity it offers. Homesteading is considered a variation of lifestyle today. It's a deliberate decision to get back to the basics, get away from the materialistic aspects of capitalism, and just take care of ourselves and our families.

Homesteading is not something that can only be achieved in rural areas; even urban people may benefit from necessary self-sufficient activities: • Purchase food products in bulk or on request, and conserve them by canning, freezing or drying.

• Buy a sheet of eggs and/or meat (standard size chicken or bantam). There are other places where you can get a chicken or two.

• Small greenhouse, and co-op the area, selling various vegetables.

Any of our production expenses were purchasing ducks, seeds, canned jars, and supplies. My hot water bath and pressure canner had come from someone who didn't need them anymore. When it comes to the preparation point, the best advice I can offer is to think frankly about what you want to do. You may be shocked at what some people stashed in their attic and ready to readily share. Check your local magazine, farm sales, yard sales, and even try to place an ad in a free or reasonably priced magazine for your needs.

If your chickens and seeds have been purchased, feed and water (if you're not on a well) would be your only expense. Saving the seeds will ensure your garden next year. Allowing your hens to hatch eggs would fill your supply up again. When it comes to reusing products, be imaginative. We use our unrepairable cooler to hold our milk, a bent fan stand for a sprinkler system, and split hoses for deep soak water. Save your glass jars to store dry goods in, and launch the seedlings with milk cartons. Just remember: this isn't white trash, it's creative, frugal and eco-conscious.

My father may be particularly extreme when it comes to an easy life. We are building a new residence, a green shelter. Using only locally produced and recycled building materials and constructing them ourselves will save us more than half the cost of paying someone else to build them. Our out of pocket costs would decrease significantly with a fire pit, indoor water cooling systems (air-conditioning), and going solar-powered.

Any other ways to cut expenses are: • Digging a timber lot and building a wattle fence • Buying fruits and vegetables from a "U-Pick" farm • Cooking your own noodles, juices, vinegar, wine and coloring • Cooking your own soap • Producing your own yogurt and cheeses These items take time and effort, so only preparing your own meals from scratch can save you. Using rice, eggs, and water to produce your own noodles would cost you less than purchasing the same amount in the premade models. It can be said of most of the products you can make from scratch; the base materials are cheaper as compared to their comfortable counterparts though at first being more costly. Though homesteading can often seem overwhelming, it can both save you money and put your family closer together. Self-induced family fun at home is just another basic advantage of living. This also comes with optional educational opportunities never offered in a program of public schooling. For free or discounted classes for you and your children, check in with your local extension office. Take a drive around the country and search for hand-made signs that boast of selling merchandise, they will lead you to a wealth of experience and new friendships. The modern home structure isn't for everyone. Nevertheless, following some of these ideas and adapting them to your own life will make a big difference between how you see the universe and how it impacts your wallet.

You don't have to drive into the center of nowhere and stay on the acreage to support "homesteading." It can start in a community, an apartment, or on a small plot. Everyone should become a homesteader. It is more than just getting-to-the-land. A homesteader is one that is less reliant on others and is more self-sufficient.

Homesteaders practice subsistence farming and frequently grow their own food, which they cultivate in order to last through winter. Even skills such as canning and pickling are important for homeowners.

We also make their own clothes, textiles, and other crafts. Either to use inside your own house or to offer to produce any extra money.

Because of its separation, both physically and socially, Homesteading differentiates itself from life in a commune or community. Usually, a homestead only houses a single family, or at most, its extended family.

When a municipality typically has a community of people living together who share obligations and belongings but are related only loosely.

Homesteaders prefer to lead a more solitary life, and can only go into town for provisions or see friends once a week or so.

This is particularly true for homeowners who chose not to have a job and have all the money they need to pay for taxes and other work-related expenses on their own property.

Homesteads are much more likely than the average home to rely on alternative energy sources, such as wind or solar power.

The notion of going truly "off-grid" is, in addition to raising their own crops and animals, a huge attraction to many homesteaders.

Imagine not wanting to pay yet another gas or power bill! In certain cases, you will also be charged by power utilities for any surplus energy you produce, which you will then sell back to the grid.

Chapter One

<u>What Is Homesteading</u>

Homesteading is more of a continuum. The broadest concept, after all, is that it is a lifestyle with a dedication to self-sufficiency. It may include growing and storing food, using the sun, wind, or water for your own electricity; and even producing your own fabric and clothes. Some homestays never want to use money; they want to make or barter for anything they need. Some may take a more cautious approach, and while striving to support themselves with as best as they can, they may be comfortable having some resources and working for pay — either as an end target or during the transition to homesteading. Urban and suburban homesteading is a type of homesteading; people living in the city or suburbs may often find themselves homesteaders, and seek to cater for their own needs within the limits of a small residential house and yard or even a small town estate.

Homesteaders don't inherently all have the same homesteading beliefs and motivations and can be a mixed group. Some may be retiring from a lucrative career that enables them to have the money to invest in the infrastructure needed to support themselves fully on the land. Many can come home with little, building a scrappy refuge to provide for themselves in the face of economic hardship. These two situations might look very different, yet both are considered homesteaders.

Benefits of homesteading

Homesteading has a range of legal and financial advantages, including the ability to improve your quality of life, including satisfaction.

1. Homestead Exemptions Homesteaders can make use of something called an exception for homesteads in some US states. This allows homeowners to hedge from creditors and taxes the value of their home and property.

This profit always carries on to a partner if the householder dies. Homestead advantages are for your and your spouse's life, as long as you continue to own the house.

That means homesteading could theoretically give you something called protection from forced selling. That ensures that whether you default on a loan or other obligation, creditors can't compel you to sell your house to pay your debts.

That does typically not shield you from different forms of loans, such as defaulted property taxes or foreclosure on mortgages. Some states allow you to exempt all of your property from property taxes. For other instances, you're protected up to a reasonable sum, like the first $50,000 to $75,000 of the appraised value of your house.

Given that exemptions from homesteads vary too widely from state to state, you can consult a lawyer or accountant before making any financial decisions relating to your property.

2. Safety Getting the right to your property and house provides a better sense of protection for certain homestays.

With reduced expenses and taxes, and the freedom to be self-sufficient and live off the farm, homesteading will give you a sense of stability.

By living the lifestyle of homesteading, you would, of course, have lower bills.

Homesteaders continue to have smaller wages, but they do not even have to work a traditional job because they have significantly lower expenses.

3. Homesteaders congratulate themselves on finding a piece of land to call their own. Most couldn't picture renting a little apartment, wanting to get their property where they could take care of their lives.

4. Less stress Like most people living in the region, homesteaders describe experiencing far less weight than those living in noisy, busy cities and urban centers.

Imagine the sounds of birds chirping and cattle circling your house, instead of heavy cars and police sirens.

5. More Environmentally Aware Homesteaders are more closely linked to nature than those living in the area. They know where their food comes from because they always produce much of it on their own.

As a result, they have an opportunity to take better care of the environment and to make sure that their agricultural activities are safe.

This means they will continue to support their land for the rest of their lives, and hopefully, also their children's lives.

6. Good Physical Health Running a house needs much more physical work than a job in the workplace or more employees in the community in that case.

Combine this with the fact these homeowners usually consume balanced organic meals they make themselves and have much less ability to indulge in packaged foods such as pizza or chips. Less tension, daily physical fitness, and a balanced diet are all key factors in staying well fit into old age, and enjoying a long life.

7. Improved self-confidence Building a homestead would take a whole range of new skills and interests you've never had before. Such new skills will allow you to become more able and self-sufficient. And as a result, your self-esteem and self-confidence will undoubtedly grow significantly.

It's not easy to home settle. There's a steep learning curve to actually learn all the new skills you'll need. At first, it can be intimidating and maybe even frustrating. But all of these struggles will help you develop into a stronger human being. To know that you are self-sufficient and completely in charge of your own fate is a very rewarding feeling.

For certain homesteaders, civilization and the power grid could vanish tomorrow, and they will still live the same lifestyle exactly.

8. The Bonding Homesteading family will get the family back together. Imagine no longer wanting to go to work at a workplace all day.

Instead, alongside your spouse and children, you can spend your day doing chores and taking care of your house.

That means a lot of chances for each other to talk and enjoy quality time.

Homesteading does not build the ideal household automatically. When you choose your room, you are also likely to have disagreements and time.

But after it's all said and done, a family who spends time together during the day and sits down to share a meal together is likely to feel closer to each other because of it.

Disadvantages of homesteading

We're going to continue the negatives with something that might not be that bad, but in certain people's opinion, it may be a downside; the smell. If you live in a rural area and want to buy your animals, you will end up with the scent that goes with them. The lovely scent of manure in your home can fill your days, and some people can't handle this. There are air diffusers and other items that you can purchase to try to block these smells, as you can see on www.aromatech.com. However, if you have a sensitive nose, it can take a while to get used to and feel fairly off-putting.

Another big downside to living in a homestead is that you're completely cut off from modern society. This ensures that you do not have access to a host of items that you're used to having close by. Rural life means you don't have access to shops and quick treatment. Still, there's the entire problem of the internet and phone as well. It's difficult to get broadband delivered in remote areas, which means you might pay for the internet that's bad, losing a lot of time.

Finally, living in a homestead requires a lot of hard work and commitment. If you want to devote yourself entirely to this way of life, then your days will be filled with physical activities requiring tons of resources. It is not as laid back as you would have thought! It requires careful preparation and an understanding of how to stop overwhelming.

Knowing the pros and cons of living in a household will help you make the best decision when it comes to homesteading.

At the end of the day, some people suit this way of life better than others. If you don't have any connections to the city and want to stay away from it all and start being more self-sufficient, then it's okay. But, if you rely heavily on digital technologies, the internet, and getting connected to it all – then it's definitely not perfect for you!

Reasons to Homestead

• You see the potential destruction of the coming modern society. You hope that even if modern luxury goods and systems collapse, you should be prepared to live as "normally" as possible.

• To reduce the amount of electricity required and use solar, wind, or hydropower to reduce or even eliminate dependence on the grid that may collapse at any time.

• Be good at growing and improving your own food to ensure that after the grocery store shelves are empty or food rations are implemented, you and your family will have a food source.

• Reduced dependence on the government, which appears to be acting in ways that are increasingly not in the best interests of its citizens.

• Avoid high food prices and high utility costs.

• Avoid the impact of genetically modified organisms on food, and more organic diet

• In order to escape the false American dream of work, you hate to have a property that has little time to own (large house, limousine, swimming pool, camper, etc.).

In some ways, we are lucky that modern house fixing is not all or all the adventures of those early house fixers. At least not yet. Those who wish to become housewives today can do it in stages and can choose how far away from the dependents we want to be. For most people, choosing to be self-reliant or disconnected from the grid does not mean getting rid of the shackles of modern society, but more of being able to live "normally" when needed.

Reasons Not To Homestead

I'm not going to lie and tell you it's just rainbows and butterflies. Heck, little house on the prairie had a heartbreak share of it. Here are the two reasons I'd advise anyone away from home: IT'S HARD WORK; the weather is not waiting for you; the babies are not waiting for you. You work 10 to 12 hours a day, putting up fruit if it's canning season. When it's down, you're chopping down firewood before you allow your weapons to go. That is a lot of hard, manual labor. And while this labor may be healthy for you, the days you want to leave will be coming.

IT'S HARD Not just physically hard, but it's mentally hard. It is never easy to lose one animal. It's never easy to see one sick animal. You're going to waste endless hours and money growing a garden, only to have squash beetles mow it down. You're trying to raise a flock of 2-day-old hens – placing six months of caring, treatment, and food in them before they can begin laying – to get them wiped out by a predator.

The storm floods. The heat is just going to scorch. Animals are expected to die. That's going to disrupt everything. You're going to get sick or wounded and watch something collapse. So the following day, you are going to wake up and try again. Why? For what?

Tips On Homesteading

Are you new to building your homestead, or are you talking about building your own? Know from others, and stop making repetitive mistakes. Check out some of the best advice from experienced homesteaders for those considering beginning a self-sufficient homestead.

Many people who get discouraged and exhausted by homesteading take on more than they can do adequately, then feel stressed and stretched too thin. Set your eyes on a few pretty good targets each season, instead of distributing your resources through several objectives. You could end up broken and fractured.

Try using a book called "The Weekend Homesteader" to handle tasks one weekend at a time rather than biting out more than you can chew. Several subjects include: • Setting goals for your small farm and household • Setting livestock to raise • Designing your farm is perfect for you?

Are you cut out for being a homesteader? Consider long and hard before you start on what is a love-work. Be willing to go through long, hard hours of manual labor, always frustrating and unpleasant, for the pure pleasure of being able to fulfill your own needs. If like most of us do, you've grown up in a western culture, that can be a big transition and not one that other people can quickly achieve.

Plan for any income While you may initially fantasize that you will supply you and your family with anything you need and never pay a dime, that's not true. You'll have to realize that you'll have expenses that will need capital, particularly when you move to a self-sustaining homestead.

Consider the way you enjoy living, too. Will you want to go to the restaurants or go out to dance? Will you love traveling or watching cultural events? You'll need some money to afford life-long stuff you can't swap or make yourself.

Eschew Debt Borrowing money goes against any idea on which the aim of self-sufficiency is based. Typically speaking, people who wish to be homestead tend to be able to disengage from the financial system and work as little as possible for income. Instead of using currency, farmers grow their own crops, and maybe swap for things like clothing and other products that are needed.

Keep The Expenses Minimal This is relevant when contemplating the properties you own (most people who want to purchase their own land or house). Will you buy land with cash and even build a house with cash on it yourself? Or are you going to purchase a home that is already constructed on some acreage? If you are considering buying your homestead property on a mortgage, how are you going to cover the mortgage? Will you pay it off in a shorter period than 30 years?

Remember how your house will be heated and cooled, and how it will provide electricity. The use of renewable sources of energy such as sun, wind, or geothermal, will substantially reduce the expenses. Many homesteaders refuse to be "on the grid," as a vital aspect of their self-sufficiency ambitions, preferring to supply their own electricity. You will need to spend some time on your homestead determining whether you will be caring for these needs.

Embrace Simplicity and Give Up on Aesthetics. You have one goal, as a homesteader: self-sufficiency. The hours you spend keeping things beautiful are hours you should be doing practical stuff to achieve your self-sufficiency target.

If you place pressure on yourself to make your household look like it belongs in "Great Homesteads and Gardens," when doing all the required tasks in a day to manage a home, that's an impossible task. If you don't excel you are likely to get discouraged and exhausted. Let go of the lingering commitment to items that look neat and coexistent. It'll help you obtain more. Around the same time, if you're chugging along, making good strides towards the overall target of self-sufficiency, not exhausted, and being able to keep stuff tidy and safe to boot, then perfect. The point is not to fret about it.

For a homesteader, a life of comfort and glamor is not in the cards. Homesteading is all about the belief that you are not helped by exchanging time for money, as well as using your resources to provide specifically for your needs. Simple life, or life simply on earth, involves growing one's belongings and costs and learning to be content with only satisfying your needs, and letting go of wants and consumption.

Time Worked Means Self-Sufficiency If you hate the hours spent nurturing cattle, canning vegetables, and cutting wood — then it's not for you to be homesteading. Alternatively, imagine the end aim to be a hobby farm where your aim is merely to appreciate the farming pieces you don't hate, without self-sufficiency. Or perhaps a small farm is the right choice, where you focus on both earning money and farming.

Separate time in your mind from money. Sure, you would have worked for maybe $15 an hour, but then, by raising your chickens, you only worked the equivalent of $5 an hour. The entire argument is that you have lived on your own terms with yourself, and you are building something that goes deeper than exchanging your time for an hourly wage.

Roll Comedy With the Punches is sweet. Laugh, every day. Do not go into homesteading on a big horse and feeling that you are equal to everyone else. When things go bad with the chickens pooping all over the front steps, and the foxes start targeting your hens, try to maintain calm.

You'll need to take it easy on yourself and be fine if you don't meet your goals as soon as you think. Sit down and restructure your plan to reflect new goals and new timelines when needed. All are flexible. Enjoy the process of getting a little bit of self-sufficiency at a time.

Chapter Two

Different Homesteading Styles

There are several different forms of the home structure. You could have

• an apartment residence

• a smaller residence

• an urban residence

• a more substantial, more traditional house.

Let's start dreaming about what each of these homesteads would look like:

APARTMENT HOMESTEADING

This might make you giggle as you imagine what a typical home with lots of land and livestock looks like. You then turn it into an apartment.

But note, homesteading is also about becoming fully autonomous. Sometimes people want to maintain their modern lifestyle, but while doing so, try to be a little smarter about things.

So if you'd consider becoming a homesteader in an apartment, some things you could do are:

1. Grow up a container garden. Yes, some of your own plants can still grow in an apartment. What you would have to do is plant whatever fruits and vegetables you want to grow in containers instead of tilling land (because most apartments don't have that option).

You can then put them on your balcony and let them produce. You could even go as far as putting a small greenhouse on your balcony so you could grow things up into the year long.

2. Raising small animals, You might think I'm nuts, but just listen to me for a second. If you have the landlord's go ahead and enough room on your balcony, you can raise two hens. Currently, plenty of people raise chickens in apartment dwelling areas because they are a fantastic way to get fresh eggs, but they don't need a ton of space.

You could also try and raise a few rabbits. Neither will they require lots of space and could help you grow plenty of meat per year.

3. Conserve your own food Whether or not you're raising your own crop, you can also conserve your own. If you cultivate a container greenhouse, you might comfortably store your harvest by practices of canning or freezing.

Let's say, though, you can't produce your own food. You should head to a local supermarket instead. When food is on offer, load up on your own and conserve it.

Even I have been dealing with some crops for several years. I go to locally owned generating stands or small farmers to buy and can purchase products very easily from them. And my family already has what they need, and I don't have to rely on the grocery store for that.

4. Grow a garden of herbs Herb gardens take up very little area. In that way, they can be born in your kitchen room.

5. The explanation is that you don't always have enough storage capacity, let alone actually have floors.

Yet community gardens are growing in other neighborhoods. You will invest in this garden, help fund it, and even get to take part in the harvest.

6. Have as many pantry items as possible; I did not know this is what I was doing at all when I first embarked on the journey to homesteading. I always felt that I was frugal and was trying to save some money. One of the first moves I took was to make my own Pantry Staples.

And you should do that only if you live in an apartment. Make them yourself, instead of purchasing processed foods. I bought bulk sugar and flour.

I would then be making my pancake mixes, cookie mixes, etc. I made my own butter, a sour cream, buttermilk. Ultimately, I did everything I could make.

7. Cook from scratch That was another of my first steps to being homesteaded. I avoided buying convenience foods. I then had to cook straight away. This was cheaper, typically safer, and smelled way better too.

And if you're in an apartment, it doesn't even take too much longer to cook from scratch and is something that everyone should do regardless of how much space they have at their fingertips.

BIG AND SMALL SCALE HOMESTEADING

These are the traditional homesteads you would consider as. Many of these homesteads reside in more remote areas where the owners have 2 + acres to turn into their dream home.

Fully, I personally live on a small-scale homestead. We have two hectares and use it to cultivate a big garden, an orchard, a berry field, grapevines, two greenhouses, raise bees, raise rabbits, raise chickens and ducks, and goat. And we have space leftover still.

The main downside to small-scale homesteading is that in the winter months, you have to buy some of the food your pets require. I don't have enough room, for example, to grow all the hay that we need. I might allow the animals free run during the winter if push came to shove, and gnaw on my turf.

Still, I buy hay from local farmers, for convenience.

If you live on a larger homestead, though, you could be self-sufficient (like I am currently), but you could still provide ample space to supply your animals with all the food. Our house is already on the market, and for that same reason, we are planning to move to a large-scale homestead.

Larger-scale farmers, too, often have the big livestock.

So these are the places you will attain self-sufficiency with no question because of the amount of land and services you have at your fingertips.

URBAN HOMESTEADING

Urban homesteading is what got me into homesteading. While I was searching for all kinds of ways to save money, my husband kept sending me videos from YouTube of all those self-sufficient families living in subdivisions.

This was when it struck me. If they can produce a 1/4 acre of all their own stuff, why can't I do the same on 2 acres?

Many have smaller gardens to feed their relatives, a small flock of hens for fresh eggs, a handful of ducks for the same purpose, and based on HOA rules; some can also get away with keeping small animals like rabbits and goats.

Homesteading is really, as you might claim, a state of mind. No matter where you live. When you want to be free (even just a little) in the consumerist way of living, you can find a way to do it.

How To Start A Homestead – Step By Step

Instead of making one huge jump, you should slowly change your lifestyle over a sequence of steps.

Step 1: Make sure this is what you truly desire. Most people have a glamorous and idealized view of what homesteading is like. You also should avoid worrying about the daily tasks and duties that would be like if you want to become a homesteader.

For a fact, taking care of crops and livestock is a time-consuming and physically exhausting job, and not everyone is cut out for it.

If you've got a spouse or partner, you also need to make sure they're on board 100 percent and that homesteading is the kind of life you're both looking for.

You'll need to sit down and speak freely and frankly about what you're looking for when your partner hates the thought of having their hands dirty, so it would be very tough for you to lead a homestead lifestyle.

If you have friends or family who already have their own homestead, see if you can spend a couple of days helping them get a feel for what lifestyle is like. And be sure to ask lots of questions for them.

Step 2: Set Expectations For Yourself If you adopted Phase 1 and found that it's not for you to dedicate yourself to taking care of a full-time farm, that's cool.

You can still practice homesteading without selling anything and moving to the country and have a healthy lifestyle.

You can also start a vegetable garden in an urban environment, get a couple of backyard chickens, and start raising your own produce.

Only sit back and work out just what the priorities are.

• Would you like to reduce your carbon footprint by a given percentage?

• Want to stay on the grid, partly on-grid or completely off-grid?

• Would you like to grow cattle, have fruit trees, or anything else that would need more land?

When you know what you want, you'll know exactly what will become of the next move.

Step 3: Decide where to stay your ambitions in Phase 2 will help you assess the size of a property you'll need. If you plan to have a full-time or part-time job still and only do homesteading as a hobby, then you will probably be able to get by in an urban or semi-rural environment.

If you're trying to house your full-time work and lifestyle, you're going to need enough space to grow all the vegetables and fruit you need, plus space for goats, pigs, or any other animals you choose.

Besides finding out how much land you like, you'll also want to set guidelines for the general region you do want to live in.

Are you all right living in an ultra remote place, or would you like to be just outside the city?

Be sure that any land that you look at would fit with the sort of homestead lifestyle that you are seeking to achieve.

For example, if you're trying specifically to grow crops, then very sandy or rocky soil can make it harder.

Particularly little issues like having to take a long walk down to your mailbox every day, or commuting once a week to the local post office, maybe more than you felt you were signed in.

Evite the urge to suck up more than you can chew. You don't need to get 100 acres, or just 10, of your dream homestead.

2 to 5 acres are always more than enough for a single family to have everything they need. Anything bigger than that, and you might think it's even more complicated to hold than it's worth. During the planning stage, some significant homestead considerations to bear in mind include:

• Water availability. Would you have streams, rivers, or wetlands nearby, which you can use for Water? Is there a well on the estate? How much rainfall does the place get annually?

• Land protection. If you grow your own food, you don't want to live somewhere that's prone to drought, and you don't want to be close to oil fracking sites or other potential health hazards, either.

• Empire. Often the society of which you are a member is just as important as the property you are buying. You need to make friends with people in your city, and network with them. If they have different religious or political beliefs than you do, it can be easier to blend in with the group, especially in a small village.

• Fired. If you have children, is there a nearby school? If not, you would need to get them homeschool.

Step 3: Make A Budget Getting a well-thought-out budget is vital to homestead, particularly if you're willing to give up a stable job to become totally self-sustaining.

If you purchase land and houses, it is vital that you do not use any of your savings to buy them. Otherwise, you're not going to have any funds left for repairs, upgrades, supplies, or other items you need.

As a general rule, any updates or upgrades to your property will be prepared to cost 50 percent more than you otherwise plan, which could take twice as long.

When you give up a career for a more self-sufficient lifestyle, you'll need to think of those plans to produce money for yourself.

You're also going to have to pay property taxes at a bare minimum, and possibly insurance as well as stuff like a telephone or cable bill.

In case of an emergency, you may always want to have some insurance, such as whether the boiler fails or a family member gets sick.

Having through income sources from your homestead is wise. You should try selling fur, milk goods, extra fruit, and items like producing soap or other crafts.

And if your crops all fail or you figure out that there's no need for one form of revenue, you've got something else to fall back on.

You clearly don't want to grow that thinly on yourself. But to have 5 or 10 separate items or sources of revenue is not all that unusual for homesteaders.

Step4: Start Small You don't have to wait until you get to launch your dream farm. You will instantly continue your journey through the homesteading. A lot of homesteading is a lifestyle and a mentality, as opposed to where you live.

Whatever the case, this week, you should start working towards a more self-sufficient lifestyle, even though you are staying in an apartment.

You can start cultivating your own herbs or lettuce indoors if you have a sunshine window.

Have you ever had a large backyard that is not used to grow anything besides grass and weeds?

Next season, bring in a garden or raised bed and start growing a portion of the vegetables for your house. (Sure you're choosing veggies you really like and want to eat regularly!) Do you have a fireplace you're not actually using? Time to clean and get some wood from your chimney, and start using it too. Your heating bill!

You will slowly add more and more tasks over time. Even if you just make one or two small improvements in lifestyle every year, things will really start adding up over time.

You could also start raising chickens in your backyard or beekeeping. Only make sure to review what the local bylaws are to ensure that it's first allowed!

Homesteading is about all that feels good for you. You can identify your goals, and you can do them in the order that makes the most sense.

Self-sufficient electricity might be a concern for some people, and they may want to invest in solar panels right away.

Others might not be aware of charging for petrol and power.

Some people may choose to start right away, raising livestock for the processing of eggs and meat, although some people may want not to go down that path for ethical reasons.

Step 5: Simplify Your Life Homesteading constantly always go hand and hand with minimalism and leads a more frugal lifestyle.

A big part of this is breaking out of the loop of just having the newest and latest electronics, appliances, fashionable clothing, and other items that can suck money out of your bank account but don't really bring much interest.

Less is enough for the homesteaders, so generally, there is a cheaper and easier way to do it.

You will constantly be performing an assessment of your life to see what issues waste your income, time, and energy to see whether you can that or remove them from your life altogether. Adding homesteading to your lifestyle would always allow you to leave out certain prior items. Some stuff may be clear.

Like if you are now doing hours of physical activity every day on your homestead, you can probably cancel your membership in the gym.

Many issues may be more complex, and more experience will be required to work out how to will or eliminate them from life. Step 6: Learn To Conserve Food There are a lot of different ways to preserve food, but the practice of food preservation, in general, is becoming a bit of a disappearing act. Only taking up one ability in food preservation such as canning, pickling, freezing, cold storage, drying, or smoking can help to minimize the food costs.

If you cultivate your own fruits and vegetables, then it's an absolute necessity to learn to conserve food.

By the end of the season, you'll still have much more food than you know what to do with it. So if you can't protect it, then much of it winds up useless.

You will need to find a way to avoid spoilage of your food so that you can keep your family healthy in the winter months.

Also, if you're not growing your own food, learning how to conserve it will encourage you to buy food in the season when it's cheaper and more healthy, and continue to eat it all year.

You probably know someone who's got some extra canned goods you can borrow just to see.

But if you choose to buy your own canning jars or a food dehydrator, during the first one or two applications, they will always pay for themselves.

It's as easy to start using cold storage as having a safe, dark space in your basement or under your house, where you can store stuff.

Step 7: Make Contact With Other Homesteaders Homesteading is frequently synonymous with hermits or not really sociable individuals. But the fact is that many homesteaders are very welcoming and willing to share their experience with those interested in it.

You are finding a more seasoned homesteading buddy than you will really support if you have doubts or worries at every point of the way.

They're going to learn about the environment, rising trends, rules, and plenty of other valuable knowledge you're going to need because they've actually already been through it all themselves.

And don't underestimate getting the social reinforcement of someone adopting the same lifestyle as you're there, because someone else tells you you're mad.

Through a content standpoint, networking with other farmers makes sense too if you've grown too many peppers and have too many eggs from your mate, so it's easy to barter for what you need.

Or you could also set up long-term agreements to exchange food and supplies with other producers that you don't really want to grow yourself.

At the start of the season, you might just need a plow once a year, so it would make more sense only to borrow one from a friend, rather than buying one for yourself.

Step 8: Start A Garden If you have made it this far and have not yet begun a garden, just do it!

Gardening needn't be expensive. In reality, all you need is just a few dollars for some seed packs. Dirt, wind, and sun are all free, and all you need to get going is just.

You can not get the same yield as anyone who uses fertilizer, but with just a bit of love and care, most vegetables can thrive in almost any kind of soil.

If you have no land of your own yet, sign up for a community garden, or even borrow from a neighbor or friend some land. Some people are glad to let you have some spare space they don't need later in the season, in exchange for some free veggies. If you're a gardening novice, you can continue with these ideas on small-scale farming.

Step 9: Composting goes hand in hand and planting go. Even if at first you can't afford fertilizer or premium soil, after your first year of composting, you'll make your own excellent, nutrient-rich soil.

Throwing all of your food scraps, leaves, chicken manure, and extra plant matter from your garden into the compost doesn't take much effort. It's as impossible to get something incorrectly. Just let it all decompose and brush it over once and for a while, and in no time, you'll have free soil to bring back into your garden.

Step 10: Learn To Knit and Mend Clothes When working on your farm, you are likely to start wearing your clothes when tending to your crops or livestock.

If you have a tear in your pants, just chuck them out and buy a new pair. Yet to be a citizen means to be more prosperous than that!

You can patch your own clothes for the cost of some fabric and get months or years more out of them.

A sewing machine will make things quicker and easier, but they don't need it. You can patch and mend clothes with only one needle and thread to make them last much longer, and save a lot of money in the process.

Step11: Learn To Build and Replace Sewing is a good start when it comes to learning how to fix and improve the clothes you wear. But you're going to want to extend your experience with other abilities like carpentry too.

You don't have to become a master carpenter, but you want to be a good enough handyman that if they break, you can repair stuff on your homestead without ever having to call someone else in. You don't need to be beautiful in the ideas, but they need to keep it running.

Building items like desks, cabinets, or even yourself a barn can save you a lot of time if you succeed.

How To Find Land For A Homestead

Today, using the Internet, it is easier than ever to find a piece of land to build a home. It can be difficult to sort all real estate listings to find what you want.

Before you even start looking for a home, I suggest you check with the bank to make sure you have obtained a loan.

Holding a pre-approval letter will help you know exactly how much money you have to spend on real estate and simplify the negotiation process.

Some things to consider when looking for the perfect land include:

• Property rights. Will you own the mineral rights and water rights of the property? Don't make assumptions when providing quotes.

•area. You seem to want as much land as possible. However, it is not always necessary to have more. You don't wish to land beyond maintenance. Woodland is ideal because it does not need to be maintained like a pasture; you can use firewood for heating or sale to earn additional income.

• Water. Ideally, you need at least one natural water source, such as a pond or stream, which does not dry seasonally. This way, you will always get Water.

How To Create a Permaculture Homestead

Permaculture is another way of saying "permanent agriculture." It's different from traditional agriculture because it deals directly with the environment's natural powers.

This takes into consideration the wind, climate, heat, natural plants, biodiversity, and other influences. It's simply a more systematic approach to growing vegetables and fruits.

You may be producing a monoculture on a traditional homestead. It involves cultivating a particular grain, such as corn or wheat.

That can make your crop more vulnerable to pests and harmful insects, reduce biodiversity, and can also harm your soil's health.

On a homestead of permaculture, the focus is put on observing and communicating appropriately with your land in a way that makes sense.

Homesteading permaculture respects and using variety, rather than shunning it. We are more likely to take a holistic approach and benefit from multiple crops or livestock forms that function together well.

Some permaculture farms go further and generate no waste while others do their best to conserve and support carbon and reduce their reliance on more scarce resources.

Permaculture plants are most usually organic and do not use pesticides or other hazardous substances either. We capture and collect resources where it's available, such as rainwater or sunlight.

Many small-scale homestead farms generally move towards a more development type of permaculture.

But I will encourage you to actively attempt to create a homestead for permaculture because it would help both you, your food production, and the world as a whole.

For more information, please check out some of our other posts on agroforestry, food trees, and regenerative farming.

Chapter Three

Traditional homestead construction

Trees and pebbles. When deer or other species come by, this is what we see as we look out our door. Only up our lane is a beautiful but humble house dated from the 18th century. The typical passerby can not find anything especially worthy of notice about it from the lane. It is merely a home, albeit an old one. However, the fantastic and almost incongruous part is that it's made purely from the local trees and rocks — essentially the same ones that we see out of our eyes.

It would appear that the term "simply" best fits a typical homestead building. This is entirely ineffective, at the same time. Within these old systems, there is an interesting combination of simplicity and complexity, pragmatism, and beauty, not to mention hard work.

It is convincing for the early craftsmen to gaze out into a wild landscape and see a way to create a full house from the materials at hand, with a selection of hand tools. The craftsmanship was excellent, and it endures, even fulfilling its central function for later generations of the new inhabitants.

Raw Materials for Traditional Homestead Building

At the moment — extremely necessary as it is — the whole house-building project began with one essential tool: the felling ax. This piece, with its wooden haft — preferably hickory — and metal bit or ear, is familiar enough to us today. But as with so many things that at first glance seem dull, there's just a little more to it than that. It turns out that a profile of the bit is essential for an ax to cut efficiently. Too much metallic meat on the arms, just below the cutting edge and the bit in the cutting stroke, would stall prematurely. Not enough, and maybe the edge is too thin, and may not hold well. A properly-sharpened ax in a professional woodsman's hands can be a remarkably powerful cutting weapon.

Of example, the methods of felling trees with an ax have several subtleties, so we're going to push right on to the next level of the build, where felled trees become logs, and logs become posts and beams.

Hewing

Now, most frequently in a typical sawmill, a log is a squared-up piece of wood – a post or a column. But early home-builders could make excellent posts and beams with only a few essential hand tools. The broadax was the leader of them.

At the first height, the broadax is an awkward brute of a thing. Because of its large, bulky, almost hideous bit and its comparatively thin, crooked handle, the uninformed axman could bust a gut with such a ludicrous weapon, wondering how to fall a tree. But tree felling is far from the purpose behind the innovative nature of this device. The broadax has only one intent and one intent — making a smooth, accurate edge around a log's face, and excelling at that, it's more like a chisel than an ax. Although the trees may be down and limbed, early homebuilders — housewrights — didn't want the felling ax to be lost. There will be some planning work for the broadax to do its job properly. The felling shaft helped to create chinks along its length in the wood. Instead, when the broadaxman made his move, the waste wood came off in chips instead of in long slabs, which would either run too deep or too shallow. Also evident in many old, bare posts and beams today are these slice marks from the felling ax.

A hand-hewn beam in progress using a flea market broadax from a small-diameter white ash block.

Joinery

After the research and craftsmanship that went into hewing them, the massive structural timbers would be worth more as firewood than anything else if it weren't for an ingenious way of linking them into a sturdy structure. The method is the joining of mortise-and-tenon. The mortise in one timber is simply a hollow-out hole, and the tenon is an end built into another timber to fit into the mortise. The relation looks a little like a lock and key.

For example, putting two pieces of wood together does not do any harm, without somehow protecting them. The mortise-and-tenon joints were hammered by builders so, but not with any regular nails. Treenails were used. Metallic nails are not treenails but instead wooden pegs. As the mortise was a void, and the tenon was a traditional piece of wood put into space, digging a hole between the two and pushing a wooden peg — a trunnel — between it, they would tie them together.

However, there was one more trick of all the mortising, tenoning, and tunneling. The craftsmen would balance the holes by the mortise proportional to the tenon, rather than forming the joint, digging straight through, and then putting the trunnel in. Driving the tunnel home will then draw the joint in and securely lock it in. Joiners used a metal pin — the drift wedge — to help line up the holes in the joint before ultimately driving home the trunnel.

And, ever so methodically, through this cycle of connecting columns, beams, braces, and other wooden parts, the builders assembled the house frame, all with the same mortise-and-tenon joint, or the pattern variations. They have used other common cabinet-making joints, including the dovetail, to tie in the sill members from floor joists.

Foundation

Speaking of the sill, we left out one not-so-minor aspect of the whole operation. Of course, the sill needs to sit on a stable foundation. Otherwise, any of the World's fancy post-and-beam joinery won't count for much. The building had a base.

Since rack trucks full of foundations form panels and massive cement mixers to fill the forms once in place were the stuff of the future, early builders used what a plentiful natural resource — stone in many areas was.

Native stone was always plentiful and acted as a solid base for a building. This was necessary to bring the bottom of the building down below the frost line, depending on the area and the form of soil, so that freezing and thawing cycles did not heat the construction up and down. This depth in colder climates will be many yards.

Not to disrespect the excavators — draft animals tend to be among them — and stonemasons who have accomplished the arduous and professional job of building the base, we must for the time being remain above ground and start with the structure.

Raising

With temporary deck boards in place, builders could step by step lift the principal building structure. Using such hewn timbers, artisans had built the foundation for the building's external walls, using the all-important mortise-and-tenon joints secured with trunnels. When they were finished, they raised the framed walls from their horizontal positions on the deck to their final, upright posts on the sill – each a so-called bent. There were also mortise-and-tenon joints where the bend was fixed into the sill's corners. Tying together all the tendencies yielded a big, cube-shaped container.

Roof framing

The roof frame has its own special set op timber joints, more or fewer variants of the mortise-and-tenon and dovetail ties. The roof framing has seen two separate solutions. Another saw the rafters going down to meet just at the support posts, with purlins running perpendicular and dovetailed in between the beams. The other put the rafters on the top plate with support purlins under the rafters, be it under or on the columns. The roofing boards went horizontally in the first method; in the latter, they flew vertically.

Sheathing, Siding, and Shingling

Now there is a concrete floor deck with a frame of timber rising above it. Even if we were to turn it upside down and set it up to sail, it's no more a weather-ready house than it would be a seaworthy yacht. In all, a home is a little bit like an upside-down yacht that we walk around on the deck's underside. In this case, the frame must have sheathing boards to form a hull — a roof and exterior walls. There were two simple methods for early artisans to convert round logs into flat boards. They were also interested in sawing. Another method was manual; the other way was more automatic.

The manual approach was for the pit saw, a contrivance that was, in theory, very straightforward but one that demanded tremendous operational skills. It also demanded two workers, one on the field and one down in a room. The pit was to allow the operator downstairs standing and walking space, and the saw clearance to run up and down from above. A Structure provided the above log.

The water-driven sawmill was a little like the pit saw a version of Rube Goldberg, except it, was far from being a joke or parody. This was labor-saving by replacing the pit saw's two-person crew with a relatively complex system and taking over the sewing process. There was always a kind of pit, but rather than a live pitman down there, an intricate collection of gears and the job was finished, driven by running water. Still, there was no shortage of necessary physical labor to run the sawmill. Workers had to load logs into the carrier of the saw and tend to the log placement and the technical changes and repairs of all kinds. Of course, once finished, the wall and roof sheathing had to get their final siding and shingles cover, much like every house today. The early craftsmen procured their shingles with a froe riveting them down. This involved splitting (riving) a short, upright log into full, slat-like pieces (the shingles) about the size of a chopping block. A blade mounted at a right angle to a wooden handle is the tool of choice for this task—this froe tool in an L-shaped type. The shingle maker will grasp the handle of the froe and smash a club-like mallet or maul against the back of the blade.

The rough shingles that came off the log also got their final taper from the drawknife, a device rather built like an old bicycle handlebar. The drawknife has two handles, like the handlebar, but a sharp blade is in between. The builder draws the knife to himself, using the razor to hack off some excess wood as part of the final shingle.

A white pine shingle, using a handmade froe and a drawknife. Of these, the house will require just a few thousand more.

Early siding clapboard often formed by breaking or riving. In an arrangement of other logs and branch pieces, the worker would set up small diameter logs that helped to raise and protect the workpiece. It became what became known as the riving split. The worker will hit the froe, push it into the end of the stack, and start lengthwise to work it down, finally breaking a piece of clapboard. There was definitely much more talent and complexity involved, but that was the gist of it.

One stage was to design the clapboards and shingles, and of course, another was to nail them onto the building. But once in place, those "weatherboards" were the near-final stages in making the house the equivalent of landlubber being seaworthy.

Doors and Windows

Although primarily structural and functional, doors and windows – like other early American house components – also often exhibited some style. The batten door was a staple of early American architecture, with many variants there. On one side, it featured vertical frames, on the other horizontal frames (battens). By pushing hand-crafted nails through the perpendicular boards and through the other hand, the doormaker fastened the two sides, then clinked them over with a quick turn at their ends. The nails came out, twisted, and then the pointing end reached the wood again. On the opposite side of the head, they presented almost like staples.

In addition to the nails that keep them together, doors obviously called for other hardware — namely, hinges and latches. The blacksmith produced all kinds of these things, including wide strap hinges and thumb latches.

A batten door to replicate. Such an original, old door will have the portion of the raised panel and the beadwork planed by hand; this one came from the table-saw. Latch and hinges are the high-quality, cast hardware for industrial manufacturer reproduction.

Flooring

Employees will now get the permanent flooring on the foundation structure using boards from either the pit saw or the water-powered sawmill. As with every point of the project, flooring had its complexities, and it required growing skill sets. As one thing, as any difference of board thickness may have existed, employees sometimes needed to change the undersides of floorboards where they encountered joists to make them lie smooth and real. The device that may seem strange to us today was in order for this work.

Much like we all realize we shouldn't ride on scissors, it makes common sense that it would not be a smart idea to swing a powerful, superbly sharp instrument comparable to an ax almost directly at the foot. Though this is precisely what the admin was doing, the risk was marginal with adequate care and ability.

Among other applications for the adz, the adz was the device that took just enough off the bottom of the board to put it down level with the others at each segment where a floorboard crossed a joist but raised too high above the general ground point. It was mostly the pit-sawn boards which demanded adzing. With the invention of the water-powered sawmill, the saw yielded a more consistent cut down the board than could be accomplished by only the most professional pit saw workers.

Stairs building

During the early American years, stairs and finish job stairs and interior finish construction went through an evolution. Stair building was within itself an elaborate art. And in old homes, door and window casings also show the abilities of those early craftsmen of molding planes. There were hand planes to place everything on the edge of a board from a plain bead to producing very intricate and elegant moldings.

So the trees and rocks from the local countryside became a house after a lot of hard work — with no lack of talent, craftsmanship, and creativity.

Everything produced ultimately originates from the raw materials of this healthy World, of course. But for many products, particularly a lot of sharp objects, perceiving some real earthiness about them can be a challenge. It is distinct from a post-and-beam building with a brick base. The system is merely a few steps away from being a trees stand. Although the foundation stones are much closer to earth, so it's no surprise that many of us are so taken with the beautiful yet functional methods of traditional homestead building, and the fruits of those professional labors of yesteryear that still grace our landscapes, providing new inhabitants with permanent shelter from the elements.

How Do You Become A Homesteader

The solution to this question is as varied as the inhabitants of this beautiful world in which we live, so here are some ideas about how to get started: 1. Evaluate Your Homesteading Commitment and Reasons First, and focus on and evaluate the motivations for choosing to go home. You need to find out why you want to stay at home, so you can make sure it can serve your long-term needs in reality. Today's homesteading might not be the life or death struggles and tribulations it was for those early pioneers, but it sure isn't privilege either. You'll be working hard as a homesteader, and the days will belong. You would be less dependent on government bodies, and more at the whim of cycles of nature.

Homesteaders also find themselves in a continual state of learning through trial and error. You can learn how to grow your food or raise livestock, but with complexity, you have to be basically all right. Homesteading isn't an absolute science, and stuff doesn't always have the effects you're planning.

As a homesteader, you will understand and be prepared to "go with the wind" and change as needed. When feeding the chickens and the neighbor's dog could get loose and destroy the whole flock two weeks before it's time to knock them out for the freezer, you should do all right. To cope with the unexpected, you will have an emotional attitude.

You and your family will need to come together, secure the greenhouse from a late freeze, or round off escaping animals, or pick up the crop before it is ruined by the coming storm. Before you get going, it is essential to realize how dedicated you and your family should be to this lifestyle. Knowing the extent of dedication will help you decide how far away your family and you will go from the grid.

When your dedication and motivations for homesteading have been evaluated, identify the most critical concerns first, and prepare for them. If it is most important to eat organically raised food, then you would want to concentrate on growing your food and building your own livestock. If you can't bring yourself to slaughter and eat an animal yourself, you'll either have to hire someone to do the butchering or keep buying the meat from someone else instead of raising your own.

2. Analyze your current position and location. If you are going to start homesteading, it is important to know what you're going to get into. Do your study, speak to homesteading people, and determine how great a jump you can initially take. Make sure you understand the local animals, renewable energy, and farming laws and regulations for your area. You don't have to own a large piece of land to begin home structure. It all depends on what you want to do and how you want to do it.

Chapter Four

<u>Homesteading Skills You Need to Master</u>

You can see it almost anywhere on the Internet, and you will find an extensive list of recommended home stability and off-grid skills that you must have or must learn. It seems that each author finds that different skills are important.

Part of the reason for this confusion is that there is a lot of overlap in the difference between home life and off-grid life, and it is mostly ambiguous.

These terms mean different things to different people. The result is that those skill lists are often confusing and overwhelming. You may complete an article and want to know the following:

• Where do I start?

• Which skills are more important?

• Which skills should be learned first?

• If I finish all the studies, will I be doomed entirely?

The reality is that no one can write an article to give everyone a clear list of where to start and focus on energy, because everyone's knowledge and skill level, current situation and plans are different.

How to do

1. Assess your current living situation and consider your future goals:

• What knowledge and skills do you already have?

• Do you want a different lifestyle in a year?

• What will happen five years or even ten years from now?

2. It may be helpful to write the goals for each time period at the top. For example, I hope to make more preparations for emergencies within three months. First, browse our main categories. Depending on your preferences and goals, you may skip specific categories, which you can skip or read later. For example, if you don't want to kill the animal yourself, you can skip the skill list under Animal Processing. If you're going to live off the grid and have a garden, but are not interested in keeping animals, you can skip the animal health and animal processing sections.

4. View each category, and prioritize the skills to be learned in the next three months, six months, and one year based on current knowledge and future goals. Write them in the appropriate columns. If you are not sure whether to include skill, try to associate it with your goal, or just list it at the end of the section. You can always decide whether to do this in the future.

5. After completion, you will have a customized study plan to reach where you want to go. First, focus on learning the skills you listed in the 3-month column. After you have mastered these skills, go to the next column.

Fire fighting

Keeping yourself warm and dry and the ability to cook on fire is a crucial skill for any housewife. On the homestead, sometimes you may be trapped in the wild, or sick or injured animals in the woods.

• How to use a stick to catch fire

• How to harvest, split and store firewood

• How to safely extinguish the fire

• Outdoor cooking, especially in warm climates where indoor food is too hot.

• Use wood or other sustainable fuels to heat houses

• Make and store charcoal cloth to prevent fire

Collect, filter, purify and store water

Ordinary people can only survive for three days without drinking water. In the event of a power outage, natural disaster, or SHTF, natural water sources may be unavailable or contaminated. drinking water and cooking water is a vital survival skill. The ability to develop and maintain reliable long-term water sources is critical for home and off-grid living.

• How to collect rainwater

• How and where to dig wells

• How to identify and develop springs

• Build your water filter

• Distilled water or alcohol technology

• The best water purification method

Renewable Energy

The term "off-grid" usually refers to a lifestyle that allows homeowners to disconnect from traditional utility networks. In many cases, some or all are powered by renewable power sources.

For some people, this can be in the form of a natural gas generator. Still, many off-grid and even homes prefer to get all their electricity from renewable energy sources (such as solar panels, wind turbines, and even hydropower). Renewable energy dramatically reduces or also eliminates the monthly utility bills, which is more beneficial to the environment.

• The way solar energy works, the equipment needed, and how it can benefit your house.

• The way wind turbines work and the conditions required to work in your homestead or off-grid home.

• Understand the difference between AC and DC.

• How to estimate current power consumption and plan to replace the power system.

Foraging and fieldwork

These are essential skills that may require temporary or even long-term survival by "leaving the land" under any circumstances. Learn these skills to collect materials, food, and medicine that can be used to reduce the need to purchase.

Not everyone will spend time, but if you do, you can exchange what you have collected or earned to get other items that you need but do not have. Using medicinal plants can save your life.

• Identify and forage edible weeds and plants
• Identify and feed plants for alternative medicine
• Determine the difference between edible mushrooms and poisonous mushrooms
• Understand when, where and how to clear

Communication skills

In today's society, we are so used to technology that even when computers and cell phone towers fall, what should we do in an emergency, many of us will be lost entirely.

Our usual way of receiving weather and information updates may have disappeared. You may be trapped under a house or building that collapsed in an earthquake and cannot shout.

• How to use ham radio
• How to become a licensed ham operator
• Signal transmission using Morse code
• How to use gestures or sign language for silent communication
• How to use second and third languages

- How to become a leader in family and community
- How to do more work with neighbors

Animal care

Raising animals at home or in a living environment off the grid can provide generous returns by providing food to supplement the garden and inventory. Animals can also help agricultural labor and help manage pasture and lush growth. But animals need careful attention and tough work. Experts recommend that you add some animals at once and master their care before adding other animals.

- How to care for and feed chickens
- How to identify and manage hens
- How to hatch and care for chicks
- How to trim animal feet (sheep, goats, etc.)
- How to inject animals (under muscle, vein or skin)
- How to suspend rest and train animals
- How to cast cut animals humanely.
- Learn riding skills
- Training animals
- Basis of animal reproduction
- How to assist with animal reproduction (foal, kidding, lamb or calving)

• How to assess whether an animal needs home medical or veterinary care
• How to milk goats, cows or sheep correctly
• How to make your dog food
• How to keep bees and harvest honey

Basic farm management

Regardless of the size of your garden and whether or not there are animals, you always need to master some necessary farm management skills. Proper record-keeping and plan management of the farm may be the key to its success.
• Keep records and gardening catalogs
• Keep records and conduct animal care and breeding lists
• How to better manage pastures through intensive grazing
• Use all-natural pest control technologies
• How to manage pests.
• How to protect livestock from predators.
• How to cut, bale and stack hay
• Recycle and reuse everyday items to reduce waste

Vertical planting and container garden

Vertical planting and container gardens work well for small areas. Strawbale planting and lasagna gardening work well in places where soil may not be suitable.
Aquaponics is a very smart way for those looking at off-grid life to be gardening.

- Aquaponics
- Herb cultivation
- Aerial planting
- Strawbale growing
- Woodland cultivation
- Lasagna gardening

Crafting

There are so many things you will need on a homestead or in an off-grid situation that the more you know how to make yourself, the better protected you will be. Learn how to make rope from alternative materials, to make your candles, and to do simple repairs to clothing as those are essential survival skills. Other skills you learn will depend on your situation and interests in this area.

- How to repair distressed clothing
- How to make a quilt.
- How to crochet or knit
- How to dye
- How to produce your natural painting
- The craft of broom construction
- How to construct clothing with recycled fabrics
- How to design garments and handmade pieces with scratch
- How to build beeswax or tallow candles
- How to make lip balm and lotion

• How to make your paper

Money management

Financial management abilities can help just about anyone. Homesteading involves considerable investment in land, machinery, animals and so on and can never become "profitable" Off-grid living may also require devices using alternate power sources, such as solar, wind, or hydro. Get as close as you can to debt-free, and learn how to swap for something you might not be able to buy.

• The art of selling goods and services
• How to build a budget and handle resources
• How to reduce expenses to become debt-free

Personal Hygiene

Personal Hygiene to Sanitation is essential in any living situation. Weak hygiene practices may lead to illness, other diseases, and can draw rodents. For farmers and those living off-grid, the search is also for more sustainable approaches that use fewer pesticides or less non-renewable energy (electricity dependent on fossil fuel).

• How to make your washing cleaner
• How to make your personal cleaning equipment
• How to make your personal skincare equipment
• Tips for hanging and using a clothesline to dry clothes
• How to wash your clothes without power

• Off-grid grooming and sanitation methods

• Composting toilets, benefits and drawbacks

• How to construct a greywater retention device.

Start learning the skills you've mentioned under the column of 3 months, and go on from there.

Keep the schedule versatile and add new abilities when you come across them or become involved in them. You'll be living your ideal homestead or off-grid lifestyle with a little time and some hard work!

Chapter Five

The Basics of homesteading

Homesteading is about being more self-sufficient, reducing your reliance on external outlets such as electricity and retail supplies, and leading a more rural life to be safer and more your environmental effects.

Attaining those goals requires that we actively learn new skills and build on that experience.

If you're just beginning to see yourself as a homeowner or you're already living the country life, and you're ready to commit to a self-sufficient lifestyle, then think about upgrading to one of these simple homesteading and essential skills that every homeowner needs to know about.

STAYING ORGANIZED

It's a lot of work to operate a homestead! And you're going to get distracted easily if you don't get coordinated.

When you have animals to take care of, a house and a garden to support, plus kids in school or home school, it's too easy to forget little things like when you last wormed the goats.

If you're not used to having all your relevant documents, dates, and activities in one convenient place, now is the time to start learning to be organized.

Although you're still practicing these simple homestead skills, you've got less on your plate, so it's easier to apply to form a new habit.

Finding Your Cash Crops

Growing your own food is exciting, but if you've been gardening successfully for a few seasons, you may be curious about selling products or choosing the best crops to grow to make money.

Some crops that attract more attention to the local farmers' market — a juicy crimson tomato or a spectacularly speckled, uniquely shaped summer squash — but experts agree that there is no magic bullet in the choice of what to grow for farmers looking to make a profit.

"Tomatoes or salad greens are the first two items that come to mind if people really pushed me, but it's definitely not a formula to make a profit, it depends on your local market, your skillset, your weather, your microclimate, and your macroclimate." The best crops to grow to make money would rely on what customers in your region are willing to purchase, as well as the time, energy, and resources you need.

"Some people had good luck with tomatoes, but in some places you can hardly offer plants in August or September, in Maine, for example, it will be much harder to make money selling late summer tomatoes in Portland than in northern Maine, where the market is less saturated with local growers.

Instead of asking what is best to grow to make money, farmers looking to make a profit should reframe the question: in my case, despite all, what is going to be the best crop for me to sell?

Step 1: Find out what resources you have at your fingertips.

First, figure out what resources you have at your farm or home. First of all, the amount of land you have will restrict what you can expand.

"One crop that is very common is sweet corn, but the amount of space it needs in addition to pest control, fertilizer and weeding make it a tough crop to make money on, even though everyone wants sweet corn, you just need to be on a larger scale. That's one thing many farmers know the hard way. "Conducting a soil test to gain an understanding of the acidity, hardness and composition of your soil to determine which crops are ideally suited to your soil.

The resources that you have at your disposal — season extenders, for example — can also give you an edge on the sales side.

"The only way to get a premium for tomatoes is to get them on the market before anyone else, which needs more infrastructure, some farmers who have invested in high tunnels, which make it so that you can grow sooner or later in the season, and they have had very good luck with leafy greens and salad mixtures, which can be very lucrative."

"You might make the whole year, or you just want to concentrate on the season, say I teach, or I'm a nurse, so I want to be busy during the strawberry season and get it over.

Step 2: Conduct market research

The next step in identifying a viable crop for you is to do some analysis and find out what people in your area are interested in buying. It's about finding the customer and if they're willing to pay breakeven or more for the commodity, whether there's a farmer's market where you're interested in selling, spend a few weekends wandering around to see who your rivals are and what goods are already accessible.

Consider working with a bigger, more experienced farm to fill any holes in your inventory. For example, if a farm on the market mainly produces beef, you might grow garlic, onions, and mushrooms to suit the beef, maybe for their Community Sponsored Agriculture subscription boxes.

You may also visit other potential customers, such as restaurants, local co-ops, and natural food shops, to see if any holes need to be filled.

Step 3: Keep up-to-date with trends

If you're producing in small quantities for local markets, it's recommended to select a single crop so you can dominate the market. If you're creating in small amounts for local markets, it's recommended to pick a single plant. Specialty crops or niche crops, as a rule, may have more value, particularly if you only have access to one or two acres, keeping up with food trends can also enable you to fill emerging markets, particularly if you are interested in selling your produce to restaurants. The Restaurant Association publishes an annual culinary trend forecast that forecasts what's going to be popular next year.

Although it may be essential to use caution when investing in trendy crops, you can have almost too much of a market for your customer, the last thing you want is for customers not to buy because they don't know what to do with it. We've seen some of this with baby vegetables and pattypan squash. "You can help market your niche products by offering samples to your clients, supplying them with shelf-life factsheets and adequate storage for crops, or delivering recipes, but eventually, you're relying on the taste of your consumers.

Step 4: Decide your financial objectives.

To find your financial objectives from rising. How much would you like to make? Is it $5,000 or is it $50,000? Are you going to quit your job or improve your work? Starting there, function backward.

It is advised to set up an enterprise budget — the projected revenue and expense associated with the crop — before you start increasing. She said that such budgets frequently do not take into account diseases or pests or weather-related problems, but at least they can help you price your product.

When people look at various types of crops, a lot of extension services write up and have these budgets available; they're a great guide. I know that farm paperwork is not usually the most common with any farmer, but being practical about numbers is important. "Step 5: Growing up something you love No matter what you grow, experts agree that you will enjoy building it.

Selling crops is not always instantly or highly lucrative, but it must always be a labor of love.

Typically speaking, we suggest that most people do not expect the first three — sometimes, five — years of development to produce a significant profit. There is a lot of time investment and material investment that goes into growing any kind of crop. It can be a satisfying company, but you want to make sure you keep it in line with the things you enjoy doing.

Chapter Six
<u>Starting Your Business</u>

Have you ever wondered how you can turn your homestead into a thriving business?

Well, like a lot of other things, it all begins with a plan.

Yet how are you going to build a homestead business plan? How do you need to think about before you start this idea?

This is where I can support you. I'm going to give you an outline of making your business plan, but you're going to have to ask your own answers.

Yet here's what you're going to remember, and the pieces of the real homestead business plan.

And you see, a business plan is not just for someone who wants to start a brick and mortar company. It can also be useful for those of us who want to turn our land into a way to make a profit. This can also be used if you wish to make an object on your homestead and sell it on the market.

Nonetheless, I see now that a business plan really requires you to sit down and think about as many facets of a company as you can. You're required to put the ideas down on paper and sort about them thoroughly.

This also lets you look and see what your challenges might be, how you can overcome those issues before you even get going, and even what your future areas of strength might be.

Whatever your dream is, a business plan is sure to give you a better shot at making it happen because it helps you think about your idea.

Part of the Business Plan 1. Executive Summary The Executive Summary may sound pretty complicated, but it's a quick start to your plan. It's where you can quickly find and discover all your important knowledge right in front of you.

So, if you're developing a business plan to bring a family member or a friend on board, or even if you're developing a plan to see whether your idea is going to succeed, this is a great place to start. You're going to want to include your actual business name and the address where your company will be based.

Then you're going to want to include what you're looking to sell. This may be a benefit (like using your bees to pollinate specific sites), or you may be selling tangible products (such as organic fruit and vegetables).

From there, you're going to want to share your business mission or your business dream. It is where you get to know what your 'why' is about beginning its lucrative vision. If you're selling pollination, it may be because you want to see a rise in the number of bees and do your part to help keep the plants going. And if you're selling organic fruit and vegetables, your goal may be to see people adopt a safer, fresher lifestyle that ideally allows people to recognize what they're investing in their bodies instead of taking the words of big business for it.

Finally, you need to decide why you're going to make this business plan. Is it so that you can get someone on board to help you create a dream physically or financially?

But is it more so that you can coordinate your thoughts and think about an idea? Not to mention, you're going to have a place to go back to when you feel like your vision doesn't stay on the path you've planned. You should go back to this strategy and see where something went wrong and amend it from the stage at which you are at the moment.

2. Homestead Description This is a very critical aspect of your homestead business planning process. It is where you determine how much responsibility you want to take on your business.

So you're going to have to decide first whether your homestead is going to be a single owner or an LLC. Managed business means that you have no legal research completed and that the company and you are the same.

But even though it's easier to set up a single company, because the expense is smaller, remember that if someone tries to sue you for something, then your financial records, your house, because the land is all on the table. There's nothing to distinguish you from your company.

But, if you want to meet a lawyer and take the necessary steps to become an LLC or a limited liability corporation, it will be entirely different. When your business owes a debt or obligation that you simply can not pay, the business or person you owe may seek whatever is in the name of the company, but what is in your name is out of bounds.

And you're going to need to go about this in the preparation process.

First, you'll want to provide a brief overview of your company or company vision, and also explain what your business can do and bring to others. In the Executive Summary, you touched on this a bit, but here you want to go into depth.

Then you'll want to provide a summary of your product or service and also share what kind of customer base research shows you might have done.

Then you'll want to describe the market you're going to enter, an overview of the financial side of the market, as well as the opportunities for growth.

Finally, you're going to want to list your short-and long-term business goals and how you intend to make this dream a profitable reality.

3. What You'll Sell Now we're moving on to what your homestead company might actually sell to your customer base. You may want to start this portion of your business plan by providing a thorough account of what your product or service is and how the customers you expect to sell it will benefit.

Then you're going to want to do some work on your rivals. You will need to address in the section your position in the market and the advantages you have over your competition.

First, you're going to want to explore the lifecycle of your company. Products are going through various phases in which they will reach the market, expand, mature, and decline. You need to think about how your product or service can manage every stage of the process.

Then you're going to have to decide to do some research and development and find out how you can make room for your company to expand even though one product has peaked. That's the difference between the homestead being a family enterprise or a one-hit-wonder.

4. Market research Knowing your business (even for home staying) is so relevant. While we prefer to live a simple life, business is never accessible. You can compete with nearby grocery stores that are more convenient and sometimes less costly.

And you just need to learn if the business is some sort of competition at all. It is where you dig in to realize what you're up to and how you're going to hang on to your own.

Next, you need to learn the demographics of your client. Is your homestead going to have fresh, hip things (like micro-greens) that a lot of young chefs opening small, famous restaurants would like to be a repeat customer for?

Or are you selling more conventional products that could cater to an older crowd? You need to know that how you market to various age groups differs dramatically. You'll use this part of the business planning process to do your research and write down who you're looking to sell.

And you'll need to get real information about the market you're trying to break into and what the future looks like, and you'll know if your product or service has a bright outlook for the future. You would also want past, current, and future industry data to be included here. Some research is required, but the internet should have all the information you need for this part of the process.

You need to determine your rivals, eventually. This is where you'll find out who you're up against, and what they're doing right, and what they're not doing as well.

Then you will be able to take this information and apply it to the next step in the business planning process.

5. Your approach When you see people going into business, a large part of whether or not they do so depends on marketing. If people don't know about you and what your business is all about, then how do you intend to do it?

And that's a very critical part of your business strategy.

First, you need to find out how you're going to promote your company. Are you going to build social media pages to spread the word? Are you going to develop professional signage to put all over the city? Are you going to hand out business cards or leave vouchers or business cards to local businesses?

Or are you going to take out a newspaper ad? There are a variety of ways to market your company. You just need to see what's most practical for your region and your budget.

So you need to find out how much the product or service would really cost you. You'll need to learn how much you're going to charge for your goods and services. Can you think of any early promotions that could help you get people into your business? If so, you're going to want to write down those.

You're also going to need to work out the logistics of running a business. For example, if you're using bees for pollination, then you need to learn how you can transfer bees efficiently from place to place in a way that doesn't duplicate hives. All this takes thought and a lot of teamwork.

Finally, you're going to have to decide if you're going to hire someone to help you run this company. Also, where are people going to talk to you about your goods or services, and what are your hours of operation? You're going to want to hammer out all the specifics before you leap in with both feet.

6. The Organization Plan You may want to consider missing this part if you're going to do business on your own.

However, if you're going to do business with a friend or family member, then you'll want to consider giving the owners a brief profile. This will share how much of the company each person owns, how much involvement they will have in day-to-day operations, and also list their expertise or background knowledge.

Additionally, if someone else is involved, like an accountant or a lawyer, you'll want to include it in this section as well. It's a great way to keep track of who you contacted in the early stages of your company.

7. Finances We're finally going to get to the funds. Money matters when you run a company. This is the part of the plan where you set realistic financial targets for your business. You're going to need to take all the work you've done in previous parts to find out how much money you're aiming to make in the first year, the first five years, and where you're going to see your company financially in about ten years?

Then you'll chart your goals, your strategy to achieve those goals and your line of thought as you set those goals.

And now you know how to make your homesteading business plan. This is going to look different for everyone because we all have different goals when it comes to turning our homestead into a company.

Tips to Creating a Successful Homestead Business

1.Start Small: In the startup and online marketing world, you'll hear a beta-testing term. I'm a great believer in it. This means checking your planned company or how to make money with a limited number of customers first.

It helps you to see if there is real interest in people who are going to put down the capital if you're ready to move it to a larger scale, and also to see if something is wrong or needs to be repaired before it's going to be bigger or more prolonged.

2.Load from the beginning. Once we start, especially if you've given your homemade goods away for free to family and friends, it may feel weird asking for money, but you must treat it like a business if that's what you're trying to do.

With your beta-testing, you can charge a reduced price in return with people who are your first customers and understand that you're paying less because you'd like their reviews and they're getting a special discounted rate for the first time because of this.

You can want to charge the full price for your beta-testing, but only have a limited number of products for sale. Still, let customers know that you would like their reviews and testimonials if they liked the product.

It is particularly helpful if you're looking to do some kind of online sale, even if it's only on social media. Such ratings and testimonials are very important.

3. Keep records from the beginning. It's important that you keep receipts and records for a variety of reasons, but particularly if you're building a company. You're going to need those receipts and the paperwork to come tax time.

Keeping records is important for your homesteading, but particularly as a company. You'll want to keep track of any cost (so you know how much to charge for making a profit), breeding records, feeding records to see if changing the feed form would increase the weight of the butcher when it comes to livestock.

You'll want to make notes on the recipes for the cottage style company. I can't tell you how many times I made a tweak on a method and didn't write it down, assuming, of course, that I should remember, and then when I go back to make it again, forget exactly what I did.

4.Know the rules for running a company. Get out of the way in good habits. You may not want to develop into a full company, but if you do, you're going to make things right.

Make sure you have all the licenses you need, you deduct all you can (but a good accountant is worth it because sometimes people want to deduct stuff you can't, and some don't know you can deduct stuff you don't), you have insurance if you need it, and you pay all local, state, and federal taxes/fees when you need to.

Federal legislation allows you to disclose something above $400 a year in income.

5. Considerate shadowing work Say what? Most likely, someone in your field is already doing what you want to do. See if you can meet them or, better yet, work with them for a couple of days and see if you really want to do this as a company to make you feel at home.

If you're going to have a booth at the Farmer's Market, go there and chat with some of the people with boxes. What kind of set-ups seems to do well? When are they going to face the most traffic? What fits well for them? What's wrong?

Many people are going to be able to speak with you. Be frank and say you're talking of making your own booth, but you wanted to see how it went for others to get started on your best foot. When anyone isn't able to talk with you, thank them anyway and move on.

6. Understanding that when something doesn't work, I say that because sometimes we stick to things because we said we would (being a person who stands by what you say is a positive thing) but just because you say you're going to try your hand to sell handmade soap and candles doesn't mean it's going to be forever.

If you don't expand or earn enough to cover expenses and make a profit, take some time to re-evaluate. You can need to look at finding new customers or ways to market your product. You may need to find a way to get a better deal on your ingredients.

You may find yourself making good money, but you don't enjoy it. You're scared to make a product or go to trade fairs or set up a booth. Look for a way to cut stuff you're afraid of or consider not doing anymore.

Homestead Business Checklist

1. Why do you want to transform your homestead into a business?

Making money is a good excuse, but it still shouldn't be the only factor. Whether you choose to balance your economic, moral and physical wellbeing principles with your job or want a way for everybody, from toddlers to elders, to invest in the family economy, the inspiration to launch this company can direct everything from the program or commodity to quality to your consumer base.

2. Why do you build various sources of income from a single household business?

Homesteaders realize the risk of throwing all the eggs in a bowl. In addition to the threats each new company deals with, homeowners must always recognize factors outside their control: environment, pests, agricultural prices, modern farming regulations are only a couple. Think of several projects under one homestead umbrella to protect yourself and your farm. For e.g., if your farm specializes in rabbits, you will have a meat project, a fiber and pelt project, a garden manure project, and a breeding project. You may extend this to involve constructing rabbit huts and rabbit tractors, writing rabbit papers for homesteading magazines and forums, or designing your own money-making blog. If you're starting a basil market, don't just sell potted plants. Sell potted plants, spice mixes containing herbs, fresh pesto, and herb-flavored pasta. Add a different quantity of basil every year as the funds and awareness improve.

3. Which resources do you have, which resources do you need? Assets involve money, resources, expertise, skills, and enthusiasm. Don't get caught in the pit of believing that you need a certain amount of land to start your homestead company. Homesteading covers a wide variety of knowledge, goods, and facilities. If you're involved in fresh fruit preserves, you don't really need an orchard. You can buy fresh fruit from local growers, add some free herbs grown on the balcony of your apartment, and cook the preserves in your tiny kitchen. Any type of mushrooms may be cultivated in a spare space or workshop. Think outside of the box to find a way to get going.

Awareness and expertise will be picked up when you travel, provided you have adequate zeal to build momentum and resources to support yourself. Write books on the industry, marketing, and money management. Assist farming and business workshops, network with other producers, and hesitate to let the fear of failure deter you from doing something you've never done before.

Cut the costs as soon as you can. Invest any extra money into your homestead company. When you don't believe you have any spare funds at all, launch your company on a shoestring. You may start a herb company with a packet of seeds. Of that matter, you should feed wild herbs of free. Whatever you do, make sure you're serious about keeping up with it and though things get tricky. Note, it takes 3-5 years for start-up businesses to increase their income. Create a list of your investments and find out what else you need to create your dream of a homestead company a fact.

4. Who's the customer?

Your family and friends buy from you once or twice, but whether they match your ideal consumer profile, you can only depend on them for moral support. Moral support is significant, but it's not going to cover your bills. You ought to analyze the potential consumer for financial results. Were you offering it to a guy or a woman? Whose sex is that? Where is he or she working? What sort of schooling does the client have? Where's the client shop going? What's the interest of her? Where would he want to spend his leisure time?

Start with the basics and get out of there. The lower you will go, the stronger. When you finish addressing this question, you will have a good idea of who you're marketing the stuff too.

5. Will your target client have the resources to purchase what you're selling?

If yeah, it's okay. If you don't, you may either reduce the cost or build a new consumer profile.

6. Identify 2 or 3 of the desires of the client.

People are making transactions to fix issues. If you have established the need, you are really close to securing the deal.

7. Does the product or service satisfy at least one of these needs?

People can purchase a product often out of interest, but to build repeat consumers, the company has to satisfy a requirement or solve an issue.

8. What makes you and your company special from the rest of us?

It's possible to be so enthusiastic about the proposal that you ignore market analysis. If the business is already flooded with your brilliant concept, it's going to be hard to bring your foot in the threshold.

9. How are you going to sell your good or service to your customers?

The logical alternative appears to be to concentrate on your current consumer base and target your selling energies on families, colleagues, neighbors, and the nearest farmer's market. You should certainly focus some of your efforts there, but since small farms are frequently situated in economically deprived regions, consider extending your sales over the Internet.

10. Where are you going to set your price?

When you figure out what price the consumer is going to pay, you have to determine whether or not it would be viable for you to produce and sell the drug. How much money are you going to need to make? How many units do you need to sell to reach that goal? Is this number feasible?

11. Write down the marketing strategy.

And if you're not looking to draw buyers, a simple business strategy is a helpful resource. This serves as a path map, keeping you centered on the company target you mentioned. A successful marketing strategy should help you recognize possible obstacles and resolve them before they arise, as well as recognize and build on your strengths.

12. Build your identity online.

Build a blog or website with your own domain name. This makes it easier for people to locate, follow, and help you and your company.

When you realize just what you want your homestead company to be, you need to be sure that you are safe. Regulations differ by state, so it's essential that you get local details. It's enticing to leap into the market you've picked, despite what appears to be a simple common sense. Unfortunately, some of the rules go beyond common sense. Researching, knowing, and dealing with all the relevant laws can save you energy, resources, and, in certain instances, the farm, and rights.

Have an appointment with the local ag department and take the time before the date to make a list of questions. You ought to inform them what you're trying to do and ask for clarity of the laws that govern the area you're heading through.

The regulations that you get can appear frustrating and intimidating. Small farm start-ups usually do not have the money that the legislation appears to need. It's not the moment to give up – it's a moment for some fresh thought. For example, some states require you to sell eggs on your farm, but not on farmers' markets, if you have fewer than 500 birds. They also require you to butcher, process, and sell poultry meat from your farm only if you raise less than 1,000 chickens. That's all right, but you don't want anyone to drop by the farm at the chance. In order to comply with your legal duty while preserving the anonymity, you appreciate at home, suggest signing up for a CSA. If your customers have paid their CSA bill, you can schedule a routine drop-off or home delivery service.

Similarly, if you choose to market red meat, you must obtain a license to export it from your farm, and it must be produced in a state or nationally licensed production plant. You may escape the licensing obligation by letting the consumer pick up their order from the server.

Selling raw milk is illegal in certain countries and has stringent criteria in others. Setting up a cow or goat share is one of the easiest ways to cope with limits on the selling of fresh milk while also dealing with the legislation.

Building a homestead company is like every other homestead project: determine what you want, create a schedule, and do it. There's no perfect recipe other than the will to excel and the amount of effort you're able to perform.

Marketing Of The Homestead

Homesteaders also claim they were first drawn to a lifestyle because of a need to get out of the rat race. It doesn't take long to know that, even at home, you need to make a living. The economy is based on currency, and while there are a lot of items you can do for yourself or barter for, there are also a lot of things that require cold, hard cash. Fortunately, there are a lot of opportunities at home that can give you a good income while encouraging you to stay at home and enjoy the life you've created there. Unfortunately, no matter the good or service, without a stable client base, you're out of luck. Of this purpose, it is necessary to know how best to grow your homestead and to focus on the best marketing strategies for a small farm.

1. Promote The Homestead Through Word of Mouth Media Ads is the very best first move for homesteaders in small communities. There are a number of ways to do this. Next, place your logo, name, and contact information on your business card and give it out to any client. Hold a few business cards in your pocket so you can give them out anytime you get an unwelcome email.

Third, produce friendly, professional-looking flyers and put them on neighborhood news boards in local shops and colleges. Make sure the farm emblem, description, contact information, and product line are easy to read, and any dates for special events are illuminated.

Second, don't miss the postal mail! Email is fantastic, but people are so overwhelmed that they are easy to miss. You can use the tool available on the USPS platform to target people with a specific zip code. A postcard-sized mailer is a beautiful, simple, and relatively inexpensive way to promote special events such as farm days and CSA sign-ups.

2. Using Local Media to Help Your Homestead Making effective use of the local media. Develop a news release to be submitted to the central and regional press. If you would like to promote a special case, allow the paper plenty of time to visit your homestead, take some pictures and compose the post. Advertising on your local radio stations is inexpensive and has a robust demographic effect. Local media and radio stations are still competing for relevant content and are willing to support their culture further.

3. Promoting Your Homestead in Farmers Markets Participating in one or more farmers' markets is how most small farmers earn their income. Offer extra value for your dollar by utilizing the farmers' market for more than just selling your products. Offer or send your consumers branded items such as tee shirts, badges, bumper stickers, and tote bags with your farm name prominently displayed. Build promo stickers that you can add to your order. Don't hesitate to give out your business cards to you.

4. Building a website for your homestead Even if you are primarily dedicated to promoting your homestead company, you should have a website. You may set up one free of charge or pay

a nominal monthly fee for hosting and using a particular domain name.

A website performs some early research, but if it's up and running, it's a static platform. Users who land on your web will be able to show details about you, your company, your goods, and it should be simple for them to locate your contact information.

5. Write a Homesteading Blog: Whether you reside in the broader region or have expended your word of mouth advertising, a blog is your next move. It's quick to attach a blog to an established website. The distinction between the website and the blog is that the site is static, and the blog is continuously modified with new material.

If you want to start a blog, the most critical aspect you need to learn at the beginning is to introduce new material regularly. Decide whether to write an essay (500 words) once, twice, or three days a week, and then do it. Build a six-month editorial schedule, detailing the subjects you're going to write on. Attach images to of post — either photograph that you have taken or pictures that are free of the copyright that you can find online. Often respond to feedback and queries as soon as possible.

A number of self-promotion posts would encourage you to "use social media" That's a confusing idea, particularly if you've never used social networking before, so we're going to break it down a little. If you settle about the site you're going to use, there's a lot of free online support. Only Search your particular query, and you're going to get all the details you need.

6. Promoting your Homestead on Facebook is a huge, diverse platform; children, men, young and older adults utilize this social networking network, and your homestead would benefit from utilizing it as well.

Your profile image will be 180×180 pixels. This image emerges as you upload on other sites, comment on blogs, and anytime someone looks for you, make sure it's a successful one. You may also get a much bigger cover photo (820×312 pixels) than your profile image, opening you up a little on your photo choices. They exchanged photos that need to be 1200×630 pixels in resolution.

Your Facebook account needs to be social. You want readers to send suggestions, pose questions, and "heart" your content. The easiest way to achieve this is to post regularly, at least once a day, and to respond to the comments of your customers.

7. Using Pinterest: Pinterest is a big forum that you can probably utilize if you have a website and a blog. Ninety percent of the pins you share are social connections, which ensures you can use Pinterest to attract other users on your personal account.

Photos are important to Pinterest because they catch the eye of the consumer, allowing them to click on your post. Broad, small, text-based photographs are the forms of images that earn the most attention. As there are several forms of photographs — profiles, posters, buttons, and screen displays — I prefer to use

Canva to build my images. Canva is a free software that has hundreds of models for all manner of projects. Download the software, type "Pinterest" in their search bar, and pick the style you want.

If you have a Pinterest page, begin with at least eight boards and pin at least three times a day. Your pins should be programmed regularly so that you can focus on your material once a week and let it take care of itself.

8. Promote Your Homestead on Instagram: Instagram is a highly visual site that offers you an outstanding opportunity to share pictures of your farm and goods with your customers. The images will be the finest you can find, and the resolution will be 1080×1080 pixels.

The most crucial thing to note while you're using Instagram is that it doesn't matter how amazing your images are or how smart your captions are; if anyone likes them, you may not have shared them. The way to bring the content in front of users is by studying how to use hashtags. To select the right hashtags for your audience, go to the Instagram Explore page and find the hashtags that fit better with your message and company.

When you've got the right hashtags and are getting traffic, make sure you're bringing them to your specific website or forum. You achieve that by composing a convincing call-to-action in your message.

9. Collaborate with other farmers. It can sound counter-intuitive, but you will drum up a lot of personal business by

partnering with other farmers and homebuyers. If you're selling wool from your small flock of sheep, ask the local fiber artist if they'd be involved in holding an event with you at your home. If your sheep are sold as feed, meet with a professional chef. Because it's almost impossible for you to do all things with one product, it's helpful to have someone who can demonstrate one or more of the benefits of your products. Be sure it's not just getting you out, however. The individual you partner for will make a return, both in dollars and business connections, as well as you do. Network with other homesteaders and engage in group planting activities to expand the "neighborhood" homesteading.

10. Continuously Improve and Develop Your Product Line Your company, whatever it is, is not flawless. Undoubtedly, it's stronger than the first time you tried it, but it can also be changed. When you believe you've hit the plateau with one thing, thanks, and it's time to extend the product line. Customers like to be continually fooled, so you're in a good place to do so. If you have regular customers who purchase your apple butter every fall, reach out to them to let them know that you've got some new apple-based goods coming out. Ask if they can consider a sample in return for a testimonial/review that you will share on your website. Not only does the latest product range keep the clients satisfied and engaged, but it will also keep you excited. A farmer who's curious and enthusiastic about what they're doing is a far better sale than someone who's idle.

Ideas to Save Money as a Homesteader

Homestead living is a unique lifestyle that many people follow. There's a lot of work going on to be frugal, however. Both you and your properties need to adapt to suit your lifestyle. As one who lives a self-sufficient, rewarding way of life, I have a few ideas that can support you on your path. Here are few frugal living ideas you should do to save yourself money and make you become less reliant on others.

1. Keep Pallets On Hand Pallets are practically free timber. There are so many things you can do with this free supply of wood. Pallet wood is durable, it does a job, and it's cheap. The internet is full of crafts of people using pallets as their source of wood. Whenever you see pallets pillaged by a dumpster or lying by the lane, catch as many as you can.

2. Save your seeds: If you have a plant or crop that is especially perfect for you, make sure you save the seeds. By saving plants, you can greatly reduce your planting costs. Also, instead of purchasing cost plants that are already rising, start pods in your seeds early in the season. When you begin planting in early March, you'll have plants of the size of the store-bought by May, when it's time to bring them to the market. Save the time by doing much of the job yourself.

3. Buy in Bulk: As much as you try, there is certain stuff you simply can't produce. Flour, sugar, and other kitchen products are a good indication of this. I'm going to buy my flour in 50-pound pots. Because I'm making a ton of bread and other treats,

it's going easy. My 50 pounds of flour saved me about ten bucks. When I run out and have to sprint to the nearest grocery store for a fast pick-up, a tiny 5-pound bag would cost me around $3. It's clear to see that small items like this will add up. Keep your shelves full, and you never run out of food.

4. You must have chickens, I know it's not for everybody to have poultry, but the abundance they're bringing is overwhelming. First of all, chickens seem to grow quickly. Your community will be overwhelmed in no time at all. Second, you will use the eggs you need and market the rest of them. It might be a perfect opportunity to add to your profits. So many consumers are still utilizing chickens that also nearby food stores are selling poultry products in their pet shops. You may use chickens for milk, food, and a great source of income.

5. Consider Other Sustainable Animals While chickens are a great start; it is good to have other kinds of animals on the farm as well. Goats and cows, for example, provide milk and pigs to provide meat. It can be hard work to get any livestock, but it will pay royally. Forget about the grocery store that costs your arm and leg for food; you can grow your own. You learn what the livestock are doing and what their working arrangements are. Even if you live in a small area, you can have a few animals to help support you and your family. Cow milk is at a premium these days, so it's always nice to have a cow around.

6. Do Your Own Home Maintenance Every homemaker wants an adequate toolbox. When the hawk drips, you take control of

it. It is important to learn to rely less on repairers and more on yourself. If you get stumped on something, the internet is full of tips and helpful videos that will help you out. Because certain repairers will cost somewhere from $65-$100 an hour, even though it takes you a little longer, it's worth saving.

7. Making Your Own Soap and Cleaning Supplies is potentially one of the best savings on soap and cleaning supplies. These days, I'm surprised by the costs of cleaning items. A basic bottle of window cleaner will set you back about $4.00 a gallon. Why will I spend too much in the world when I can produce my cleaning items for pennies? The window cleaner is vinegar, water, and a little fragrance. Ammonia, water, and some fragrance can also be used. The spray bottle is a one-time investment of about $1.00. This is just an example of how easy it is to save the big one. Another thing that needs to be remembered is the chemicals they place in these cleaners. You will find choices that are much better for you, your colleagues, and the world.

8. Buy Meat from Processing Plant: If you have little room or resources to deal with live livestock, try purchasing meat from sources other than the grocery store. Meats have a big discount in the shop. If you purchase from a meat plant from anyone that slaughters and cooks food for humans, you will get a nice price. It is also safest to purchase beef and pork in bulk and store it in the freezer. For e.g., the lamb goes to the grocery store for $15 a

pound, but when you purchase it in bulk, you cost as little as $5.00 a pound. It's a massive saving.

9. Barter and Exchange: One of the forms people have compensated for items through the years has been by bartering and selling. When you need a new truck, you might be willing to negotiate a bargain to have the old ATV that you no longer need. You should donate your expertise or a slice of meat from your bulk stock. Don't be easy to run out and get loans for the things you need. Know how to connect with locals and get great offers. Sweat equity is also the greatest option.

10. Repurpose and reuse Recycling reaches far beyond bottles and cans. People are recycling furniture, houses, timber, and anything they can get their hands on. When you have an existing barn on your farm that has seen better days, using the wood to support you create a new one. There are so many items you can do as you reuse them. New life and character may be granted to old objects through any sort of painting and imagination. Don't be scared to try anything different. You haven't wasted anything if it doesn't work. You may even use repurposed products to barter new items.

Ways To Make Money From Your Homestead

There are countless opportunities to earn money; should you just care to think about it.

You may prefer to move out and try only to make a living from your house, or you can choose to have a part-time job in the city and work on your craft/garden when at the house.

This being mentioned, in comparison to a homestead, it is daunting to get a full-time career.

There could be goats to milk and feed (not to mention how much trouble they may get in in 8 hours!), crooked roosters to kill, and weeds to pick. There is still something that needs to be achieved. Meat, gardens, and livestock Is there a big flock of chickens? Offer any spare shells. Love to eat, huh? Begin the canning and help others fill their pantry with homemade jams and chutneys. Go down the list and continue talking about how you will earn money off your homestead!

1. Selling organic preserves: Supplying your own nutritional requirements is a good thing – but it takes on a whole new sense when you start feeding people with safe, home-grown produce. If your culinary abilities lead you to spend more time in the kitchen than anywhere else in the home, and you have more than enough experience in canning and preserving fruit, then preparing and selling preserves growing just be a spoon for your jelly.

Anyone that doesn't have time to create organic preserves for themselves can always love the special varieties that can't be purchased from the supermarket.

2. Dehydrated products: If your garden grows a bumper crop of cherry tomatoes and you don't know what to do with them, drying them is the only sensible solution.

Sun-dried, oven-dried or dehydrated, both of them work well with time and practice.

You may even market fruit leather if there are enough children nearby to carry it on sale.

3. Expand your garden. If you have a green thumb, it will be easy to produce and sell additional greenhouse vegetables.

If your garden has been built, all you have to do is plant more than you need for personal use and scale from there. Ideally, plant a bunch of perennial edibles and then, once formed, keep growing year after year with minimal input from you.

If you're not involved in offering a finished product, such as jams or dried herbs, go ahead and offer the raw product.

You might also go the extra mile to let people know why your organic produce is the greatest around you, by holding a cooking class in your homestead. 2 suggestions for 1!

4. Make dried herbs and spice mixtures. In a good year, you can harvest a lot of herbs from your garden. There's going to be so much greenery in a great year that you won't know what to do with it all!

You may start by drying your herbs, and then place them in glass jars. Attach the cool sticker, and they are ready for sale:

• oregano

• basil

• rosemary

• dill

• thyme

• mint

5. Plant extra seeds – sell seedlings If you have a greenhouse and are willing to start planting ahead of the season, customers are still really thankful for the tomato and pepper seedlings that can be planted straight in the dirt.

The explanation for this is because their tomato production is far easier, without all the hassle of waiting for slow-to-germinate plants.

Herb seedlings are always better marketed on farmers' markets because they can be taken care of indoors, and never underestimate the value of preserving and selling seeds!

6. Offer broilers or chicken eggs Growing a flock of chickens is a fun activity, but it comes with ups and downs. A bunch of chickens will leave you with almost no eggs at all, away from more than you can feed, and a lot to offer away.

Eggs are healthy and tasty, just as eggshells are. Keep plenty for yourself and market the rest to make a profit.

7. Grow and market heritage poultry Turkeys, ducks and geese are not as popular as chickens, but there is something to be said for their meat – and eggs!

Of course, it all depends on what kind of bird you enjoy and how much land you have, like exposure to water, whether ducks or geese want to survive.

Not to fail to note the most beautiful guinea fowl, ferociously aggressive birds that can be noisy at times, but with eggs that are still so delicious and wild.

8. Start a cow – or goat – share If you're sick of purchasing your milk in a plastic container from a grocery store, consider that maybe others are still frustrated with the same routine.

Go out and sell milk in glass bottles, as it used to be. Customers will enjoy it if the milk is smooth and tasty.

Most citizens don't have the property, or the time it takes to grow a cow or a goat. Begin a cow's share, and, in return for growing a calf, you will take advantage of extra milk, fresh or pasteurized.

9. Sell fresh chocolate, butter, and other dairy goods When your cow(s) and/or goat(s) start processing milk, you'll have to learn new cooking techniques and start making aged cheeses, yogurt, kefir, cottage cheese, bacon, sour cream, and ice cream.

Become an artisan cheesemaker, and you will start paying much more for specialty cheeses early.

Customers purchase baked butter and cheese for their regular meals, even if you might bake with your surplus, or even offer festive holiday dishes.

10. Beyond eggs and milk, meat is the next homestead commodity that fluctuates in abundance. You're not going to destroy every day, so when you do, the greed becomes clear! Bacon is one thing that can be quickly smoked and hanged. Sausage production falls next in terms of simplicity and marketability.

Though we have to wonder, who wouldn't enjoy an outstanding free-range beef protein snack without all the ingredients, you'll find in the store?

11. Crop grass-fed livestock If your homestead has the amount of land it takes to raise cattle, and you're able to get your hands dirty – go for it!

This does, of course, require some awareness of rotational grazing, select the right livestock for your property, and handle these big creatures. Again, if you're serious about it, it's a perfect match.

When you're really searching for a place to earn rent, it's going to be a lot of effort.

12. Plant an orchard or berry field Orchards require time and good preparation if you intend to thrive – and you do.

If you start from scratch, make sure you pick the right variety that functions well locally. Bonus points if the trees and bushes are drought resistant.

For example, when you start producing apple trees, you could sell fruit directly, invest in a cider press and make juice, make apple cider vinegar, dehydrate apple slices, or even make apple wine!

U-picking farms are family fun too: peach, blueberry, cherry, you name it.

This is not an opportunity for the faint of heart, because it requires a substantial expenditure to get going, but it can provide you with income for decades to come.

13. Offer freshly baked products If you are fortunate enough to have a farmer's market nearby and you can stick to getting there on a daily basis, you can have a relatively stable stream of income at hand.

Everything you've got to do is come up with a quality that sells. Cookies, muffins, cookies, crispy crackers filled with fresh lard or butter. Add any herbs or new flowers to the garden and render it unique.

14. Beekeeping If you have bees, odds are high that you would have a lot more honey than you will drink in a year, maybe even a lot of extra beeswax as well.

Selling honey and handmade beeswax candles are two easy ways to profit from the diligent work of the bees but don't worry about bee pollen and propolis.

15. Develop mushrooms Even if you have little space to sell to a money-making company, mushrooms will work for you.

Sell or dehydrate them new. Most of all, cultivate it because it's so damn healthy for you!

Oyster mushrooms are great to deal for beginners, switch from there to shiitake mushrooms.

Selling homestead food items: At some stage in your homestead company, you may have to comply with local food protection regulations. We can differ from state to state, from nation to nation. When you decide what you'd like to offer, check at what regulations could stand in your way.

As far as meat and milk are concerned, look at local laws before agreeing to any deal. It could be much cheaper to sell a live animal than, for example, to sell cut and dried chicken breasts. Raw milk is another issue, and many homesteaders would have a goat or a cow of their own for that same purpose.

Make it on the homestead through innovative activities. There's a lot more to having income going than selling produce and perishables. How about selling sculpture, drawing, or jewelry? Things that are not only beautiful and artistic but also practical.

16. First instinct goes to sheep fur, but there's so much more to livestock fiber than that.

Imagine the rats, the alpaca, the llama, the Pygora, and the Cashmere goats roaming around your property. They're both so lovely and versatile in terms of our clothes in a healthy way. And if you're not involved in making the fibers into fabric or felt, someone else does – and they can be found online. This being said, selling organic fleece and hand-picked yarns outside of local farmers' markets is a perfect way to make a living, as long as you're a crafty person.

17. Sell homemade finished products When you make fiber and know how to handle it: spinning, weaving, crocheting, etc., then you will gain much more for your craftiness.

Wear caps and scarves. Know how to knit and invest in a loom to create bigger parts of fabric for blankets, tablecloths, and mattresses.

Bring the meaning of everything you do, even a story, when you know the ins and outs of online purchases.

18. Handcrafted soaps, lotions, and cosmetics If you're trying to move into a stable market, create it that people use on a regular basis. Soap is something we use on a regular basis, so we can be pretty picky with our preferred flavors so scents.

When we discover the right homemade soap, we hold to it and purchase it again and again. How's that about a loyal customer?

19. Mend, sew, and make clothes. You don't need to get muddy to create a homestead profit, you can make a little extra cash just by repairing work clothes that are worked in pieces.

If you're good at calculating, you might also take the liberty of beginning to build your own designs of homestead clothes, and, of course, you might market it locally or online.

20. Tan and market hide With pigs, goats, or rabbits on your homestead, you're going to have an inflow of tan hides that would otherwise be thrown away.

They can be used to protect the benches or to hold you dry throughout the winter months. Our ancestors did it, and we must do it. If this is of interest to you, look at it more and see if you can get started:

21. Carpentry and blacksmithing: In the past, woodworking and blacksmithing became more of a man's company. Nowadays, more and more people are encouraged to take the hammer and design elegant metal objects.

When you can bear the pressure of a hot wood-fired oven, sitting next to a forge is going to be a piece of cake.

Carpentry goes well past home construction, which may also involve furniture which toy design! If you will trust in the goods you make, others would also see interest in them.

Although this method of making money isn't something you would quickly jump into (unless you possess the necessary tools), it can certainly be a profitable means of generating enough income to bring through your life.

22. Teaching seminars and courses Have you found your passion? Or is there something you're incredibly amazing at? Let people know and gage if there is any interest among locals. Spinning workshops come to mind immediately, studying how to make bread, creating ferments, and cooking lessons suit closely. You may be a professional gardener and have words of green knowledge – and a garden to show it!

If you've got homesteading skills to share, make sure you bill for them, never offer anything up for free!

23. Start a blog To be truthful, finding the confidence to start a blog is one of the easiest ways to get to know your homestead. But the fact is, most blogs are unable to make any substantial amount of revenue. This is for a couple reasons that we're not going to delve in here.

But if you think you have the right recipe for charisma, strength, innovative design, and blog strategies, why don't you try it? Blogging about home life can be a perfect way to raise your profits beyond the rat race!

24. Write a book. If you're an artist, remember that people are still searching for fresh and interesting material. Setting the internet aside for a moment, books always have a particular spot in any reader's existence. They're physical – you can flick through the covers, books can be brought out of nature on walks, and they're safe from battery life.

Even as you may have home-based teaching abilities, you might also have several life experiences to express in literature, be it fiction, non-fiction, cookbooks, children's tales, or even poetry. Books are great opportunities to spread information and move it on from generation to generation.

Self-publish or adopt the conventional path, if you have anything to say, let it go!

25. Become a freelance writer Will you come in from your lovely backyard, grateful to be out of the bright sun, encouraged to drip your face?

No matter whether you're an introvert or an extrovert, words are only one of the forms we can show ourselves. Some people are better at speaking; others are smarter with meaningful strings of words that roll off their fingertips.

If you want to compose, being a professional writer (in any niche!) may be one of the most appealing ways to make a living. Take the first measures by developing an essential website, or journal, and then fill it in with the related material.

Ask your family and colleagues, check the work markets, and send a cold email to get going. For a good professional ethic, it's only getting better from there!

26. With a camera in hand, taking decent images around your homestead can be a fairly simple way to earn money.

Setting up a store and selling prints online is one way to build a sales source, another way to sell stock pictures. Think ducks, harvest plants, adorable creatures, even a mound of manure. Somewhere, "maybe," people would like a beautiful photo of a haystack or a steaming pile of manure

27. Raise Worms

If you have a demand for your worms, then indeed, you have the foundation for a profitable company. And if you follow the attitude of an entrepreneur, anything is probable.

People will purchase them for fishing purposes, for vermicomposting, for reptile owners, and of course for gardeners who are not only involved in worms themselves, but also in worm castings.

28. Incubate eggs If you're in love with poultry, one of the easiest ways to express your enthusiasm for chicken with others is to market day-old chicks.

Invest in a safe incubator and get ready for a lot of cuteness! But before you launch, make sure you've got a crowd to deliver, then take pre-orders to make an effort worth it.

29. Build and sell compost. If you have the ground, you have the power to do it! And you've got all the room to create as much manure as you can literally. Not all gardeners are fortunate enough to get a decaying heap of plants in their backyard. Farm animals may make a major addition to the pile of aged manure (cows, pigs, goats, sheep, and chickens).

30. Cut and sell firewood While you stay at home, having a stack of well-experienced firewood is an important experience to know for life.

Absorb experience for yourself, but when it comes to purchasing and selling firewood, another person's "seasoning" can imply something different than yours.

When you have so many trees to cut down, more than you could probably burn on your own – sell it green (for less money) or season it well and sell it for more!

31. People need hay and straw for their farm animals (feed and bedding quality), even like they need it for their no-dig gardens. When you have extra sticks, there's a risk that anyone may be in danger.

Go old-school and set up posters to sell nearby, mention them in a dedicated Facebook page, let your homestay buddies know – get the message out that you've got more than enough, and people always lend a helping hand or bucks for what they need.

32. Rent your farm Claim you have the farm, but there is no livestock (or not enough) to bring it on. Start renting pastures for neighbors, or make a dedicated crop field. It's like sharing your ground, only for rent.

You set the guidelines and make sure you sign a deal for timeframes, harvests, and leases.

33. Give your homestead to gatherings. If you're fortunate enough to have mature trees on your farm and a picturesque environment, so take advantage of it!

Offer the land/garden to take pictures of marriages, anniversaries, birthdays. Please make careful to have reasonable intentions from all sides and to build a plan to cover one-off or repeated incidents.

34. Start a CSA If you consider that gardening and growing food is indeed your passion and one of the reasons to get out of bed every day, then starting a CSA (Community Sponsored Agriculture Scheme) that come naturally to you.

When you're up to the task and love building a stronger sense of culture, you're looking for results. Before you get going, make sure you're in it for the long run, not just for money.

35. Offer your expertise/tools to other homebuyers. If you have a tractor and equipment, suggest renting a tractor in the

surrounding field, and support others get crops on the table, as well as helping them out at harvest time.

If it comes to more than just income, of course, modern women are so concentrated on moving ahead that income always appears to be the only appropriate solution. Nevertheless, there are moments in life that it is more than enough to get by.

Live life at home helps you to do so many things that city-dwellers just can not do.

You've got land to walk, a greenhouse to feed on, hedgerows to forage under, trees that bear food, a cow's barn, a chicken coop, and so much more!

As long as you've got your fitness, food in the pantry, and a roof over your head, you're doing well!

Extra money is the icing on the plate.

No one has ever claimed that raising money from a homestead is going to be free, nor is it possible in a city setting. Each lifestyle has its difficulties, and all are full of ups and downs.

What's the best way to earn money for you, maybe it's entirely incorrect for everyone else, but celebrate that creativity and stand on as many feet as you can, and there's a "steady" stream of revenue flowing all year long. Often try to put aside for a rainy day.

When you start dreaming as an entrepreneur, all the challenges in the universe can't keep you off from living the homestead vision.

Ways to Sell Your Products

Find out how to advertise and distribute the goods.

Selling to Friends and Neighbors

It is the perfect way to launch direct marketing for new growers. You and your partner will create a collection of around 100 individuals you meet from college, parties, school, and so on. Have individuals like your accountant, your barber, your postal man, and your family. You will use this list for connections and, if you choose to market it this way, as a mailing list to let customers know when your goods will be available.

This is a simple way to launch direct selling, but it has several disadvantages. It takes a lot of time to stay in contact with customers and market the goods. Also, since these are your friends and neighbors, they may assume a lower price as a nice bonus. They can be reluctant to pay, too. You will tell them that if you wish to live in business and your farm to be viable, you have to make a profit. A decent amount of company is perfect for both sides.

Friends and neighbors may be more skeptical of your company. You've got to clarify just what they're having. Customers who are not acquainted with farming sometimes believe the 250-pound hog provides 250 pounds of edible beef. Instead, a 250-pound pig is expected to yield between 150 and 170 pounds of cut and wrapped beef, including ribs, hams, and sausages. If you explain to your customers what to expect before they buy the meat, you are more likely to keep a satisfied customer. Remember, an unsatisfied friend or neighbor can cause a lot of trouble.

Farmers 'Markets

Farmers' markets are ideal for direct marketing purposes. Consider marketing at every farmer's market within 1 hour of drive time. Your State Department of Agriculture is expected to have a list of demands.

The greatest benefit of selling on the farmer's market is that you'll meet a lot of buyers in one location. It's much better to market a few goods to a lot of consumers than to offer a bunch of goods to a few consumers. If you have something fresh and unique from the rest of the industry, give taste samples to the customers. Recipes highlighting the items are also a successful publicity tool.

The main drawbacks of farmers' markets are expense and time. Time spent on the market is time not spent on the crop. If you measure all of the expenses — production costs, booth prices, wages, and transportation — selling here can not be cost-effective. Count the pennies very carefully.

Test out the competition the season before you're planning to deal. See what the producers are growing and what they're not. Was there something missing—yellow or red snap beans, or heirloom tomatoes like 'Brandywine?' Speak to producers and consumers to see what needs to be improved. It's a safe place to continue.

If there is no farmer's market in your town, consider establishing one. Evaluate the ability of the client, define the capacity of the exhibitor (farmer), and create a charter — all of which are quite significant. Decide on premiums, days, and hours, and evaluate policies and venue. This takes a lot of effort and needs cooperation from the government. If you open a farmer's market, hosting special events — baking sales, parties, concerts — may be an excellent way to make a profit. Finally, the farmers' market would need the same thing you do—advertising to let citizens know it's there.

Roadside Stands

This should typically be on or near your farm and can range from a pick-up bed to a temporary shelter to a store. If your own land is off the beaten track, ask nearby retailers, such as convenience stores and gas stations, to set up a temporary stand on their ground, or pool your produce with a farmer on a beautiful road. Render your booth enticing, with bright signs and simple details.

Roadside stands will carry consumers to you at no cost. If you do well, you will transform this into a nice little farm store. For enough exposure, people might be drawn from miles away. Unfortunately, time is a detrimental element again. Time spent on a stand may be worth less than on a farmer's market (think of consumer dollars an hour) unless you are on a well-traveled route with a quick escape. You're going to have to determine when the hours of the stand should be. Is it available all day, three days a week, or just on weekends? Is it going to be open every day, or only at peak hours, while people are heading home? In certain places, the farmer leaves a can for money and lets his customers support themselves. I don't trust enough for this strategy, while it could be a reasonable way to dispose of excess inventory. Test the liability provisions for a roadside stand.

Community-Supported Agriculture (CSA)

It is a subscription scheme where the farmer signs buyers for a monthly or quarterly charge and promises to supply them with a portion of farm production for a season. CSAs are more than just a way of marketing your products: you have a definite partnership with your client, and your consumer bears the development burden of your farm. In collecting the annual payments upfront, the farmer stops investing capital and charging taxes and has a ready demand until he or she plantes something. Customers know how and where their food is made, so they obtain fresh produce at a reasonable price. Customers can even know a strong deal about environmental vagaries! Working with the CSA is fairly easy. Many CSAs have a starting list of around thirty customers. The consumer spends, say, $300 for seven months, and then gets a weekly delivery of his portion of the goods — probably around 10 pounds a week. Customers can be permitted to operate on the farm in peak operating hours to reduce their prices. Any farmers provide consumers to pick up their produce on-farm, with a rollover table where the consumer can delete the product he or she does not like and add anything else. Many farmers have an updated inventory of what they are planting; others receive feedback from consumers as to their tastes.

The key disadvantages to the CSA are the insistence of a good offer and the lack of consumers to sign up for it. A lot of people are afraid to spend money until they get some good. Many (but not all) active CSAs operate near to metropolitan areas with a broad consumer base. You don't want to establish a CSA unless you have a clear understanding of what you will collect per year and what it costs to increase it.

Catalog Sales

Value-added items are needed for catalog purchases and can be a logical outgrowth of a consumer mailing list. Beginning a collection involves a great deal of thinking and diligent consumer analysis. Printing, wrapping, and shipping the catalog — that's the easiest part of it. The challenging thing is balancing supply and demand, making sure you have the requisite materials on hand without wasting so much money or generating surpluses. When you don't get what the client needs because he needs it, you've missed a deal and maybe a buyer. If you've got thousands of unsold jelly bottles, you've destroyed your business.

I do advocate catalog purchases for anyone with many years of expertise with both the cultivation and direct selling of value-added goods. A catalog needs a significant amount of inventory. Climate factoring, manufacturing levels, and expected consumer returns call for information and practice. It may be smart to find another farmer nearby who can provide you with extra produce if you're running short — but it must be of a price equal to yours.

Shows and Fairs

A stand at trade shows and civic festivals will help your farm and boost your profits. Such booths are a perfect place to reach into local audiences, catering to both brand-new consumers and those who have always learned of but never experienced Aunt Sally's Special Mustard Recipe. You may consider offering some kind of booth exhibition — cooking, milking a cow or showcasing a craft (soap producing, spinning, felting, for example). Have maps or flyers accessible to display curious citizens how to locate your property.

Consult with the chambers of the industry of the surrounding counties, as well as the nearest extension office, to see what activities are open to you. Don't just glance at conventional farm and art exhibits. Think it from ballooning activities to food fairs, music concerts and community meetings, group conventions, and Living History functions. If there are no such events in your area, consider hosting one of them yourself.

A booth at a major farm and craft show or a state fair is the next step up from local events. You've got to be cautious with the prices. Note that you have to pay the booth charge (usually $50 for tiny shows and $250 or more for more significant events) before you make a profit. When you're in another area, you might still have to compensate for travel, housing, and food. I suggest watching a big exhibition the year before you present it to determine the interest of the client. Speak to businessmen selling related goods and ask them what they think about the series. By the end of the day, though, figuring out whether you're going to get enough clients to warrant the cost will only be achieved by doing a performance or two and maintaining clear records. Be warned that some performances are going to be fantastic, outstripping all expectations — but others are going to be dudes.

The "big leagues" of shows are food festivals and gourmet food fairs, where booths will cost $2,000 or more, plus penalties if you don't perform exactly as instructed. They are not for faint-of-heart, low-volume farmers or those without a substantial cash buffer. You must be skilled, experienced, capable, and know the manufacturing costs up to one-tenth of a point. If a customer asks what it costs you to distribute 100 six-packs of jam to 20 separate markets, you have to be willing to answer, "Yeah, I can do that for XX dollars and cents per case." U-Pick Farms U-picks is undoubtedly a "people-to-people" company. All the types, styles, and ages of people will come to your field, full of all kinds of challenges, myths, and assumptions regarding farming. They would happily express their stories as you attempt to negotiate with five people waiting to check out, a young boy trampling in the street, and vehicles lining the parking lot. However, if you are a "business guy" who feels that you should deliver items that are safe to your guests by presenting them with an enjoyable experience, that can be a perfect way to advertise.

U-picks

U-picks would do away with the expense and time of picking the crop and shipping it to the city. (Some farmers pick some of their plants and market them to rushed tourists at a lower price.) If buyers are on the field, you have a tremendous chance to offer them some items as well.

There are, indeed, also other expense factors. You ought to review the criteria for U-picking before you start: security, storage, bathroom facilities, a rundown rest place, and so on. Speak to insurance providers, other U-pick growers, and the local extension office for details. Test the county rules, too. Think, too, about the issues of having a large number of people to go to your farm — consider fence location and defense, for example. Again, it's good to do your homework and to talk with other U-pick farmers and your extension service. You'll need to provide novice pickers with tips to may crop damage. There will also be several "farm tastings" free of charge. However, they will deter large use. Allow parental oversight of children — you're not a babysitter (unless you choose to set it up as an additional fee). Many farms need phone appointments, while others only need drive-bys. The phone enables consumer numbers to be managed by output but needs further ads before you have a daily customer base.

U-picks used to market only cans, but most instead prefer to sell by weight. Accurate measurements are, therefore, important. It's better to get a big populated center within 45 minutes' travel distance unless you have any creative ways to bring visitors to your house. At Persimmon Hill Farm in Lampe, Missouri, Earnie Bohner runs a U-pick that is just over an hour away from every big city. But he's on a path that leads to a park, and a number of parents are heading down to see their children drop by. It offers homemade muffins and fresh berry smoothies, plus its unique berry and mushroom products (dried berries, mushroom sauce, and berry barbecue sauces). Its special items and a friendly farm act as a visitor magnet. He's still got tour busses going.

Food Circles

A food circle is a sort of connection between a CSA subscription farm and a cooperative. A small number of farmers and those in the town pool their produce — usually, one farmer for every ten non-farm families is a reasonable ratio. Supporters might pay a premium to enter, and certain groups might require a deposit. A closely organized food circle would have a delivery location (maybe more than one) where the food is distributed regularly. Members are purchasing the goods at the sales center. A consumer who may not purchase sufficiently over a certain amount of time (monthly or seasonal) may have to pay a fee. A poorly organized food network will only get citizens together to exchange or barter their products on an informal basis.

The biggest downside of the food system is that a lot of individuals have to be interested in initiating and holding things running. A farmer can consider a lot of his time focused on corporate matters. It has an advantage over cooperatives in that a fixed amount of output is not required by a supplier, and an advantage over CSAs in that the consumer does not have to spend as much capital in advance; this allows it simpler to draw consumers. Farmers may not, though, be able to change the price of their products. Many food circles set a reasonable price on all these items, bundle them, and award the farmer an amount of money equivalent to the portion he added.

Grocery and Health-Food Shops

These might be decent markets for your goods, but you'll be selling them wholesale, and you need to transfer other items to make up for your decreased profits to additional time to drive. Although useful, every bulk selling will be a tiny part of the overall revenue value.

Stores can be tough to get into because they do not already sell local products. Seek to promise them those numbers, packaged the way they prefer — they could be more manageable. For example, make sure you're going to be willing to produce the sums you pledge. Sales of sales can be a way to get the goods in the market. They do have the benefit of earning you better earnings, but you're going to have to waste more money on presentations and accounting.

Restaurants

Again, this is not a discount market, but you can get rates marginally higher than wholesale. Target specialty restaurants with chef staff: they would be more involved in purchasing fresh produce. We seem to be really different, too. It's better to speak to the chefs before you grow up and figure out what they expect and what amount they're going to use. Bring the free tests so that they may try. Many chefs may be a little temperamental. Promote their transactions with one-sheet articles and quotations from food fairs and gourmet publications. If you consider a chef willing to try your product, cultivate one or two new herbs or vegetables every season and offer them as samples. Any more information on marketing to restaurants:

• Make sure everything you deliver to a restaurant is safe and appealing. Dirty produce is a fast way to ruin your profit.

• Restaurants should be situated in a tourism destination or adjacent to a significant city. Otherwise, their amount may not be worth the time and energy.

• Seek to get a range of restaurants as clients to produce that is used in a wide variety of dishes. If the profits are focused on items found only in the chef's special house or in a particular meal, you'll be in danger if the dish shifts.

• Schedule the times of distribution. Unless the chef can't make his specialty when he needs to, you could lose him as a client. Give your number to the restaurant for rush orders.

• Guarantee, above all, that the quantity demanded by the restaurant is supplied. When the chef has called for ten items, don't hold six. Never give you something you can't offer.

It is necessary to determine the amount of market possible for each of the items. I was selling trout and catfish to restaurants when I began my aquaculture company. I figured out, however, that I was offering ten catfish with every trout since there were just enough luxury restaurants in my region to use 25 pounds of trout a week. On the other side, I delivered between 50 and 100 pounds of catfish a week to many "home-style" restaurants, and these fish did even better in grocery stores. Soon, I lowered the trout and grew just the catfish.

Community

Community Pools and Classes Private Pools are mostly sold out. They are simply a group of farmers in the area who agree to sell to each other and to promote each other's businesses. A farmer may refer a customer to someone else in the pool if he or she is out of what the customer needs at the moment or if the customer is looking for something a little different. This program also helps the consumer to make further decisions. To go further, farmers can join together to sell their stock as a group in the selling barn, or to business searching for greater numbers than a single farmer can afford. When this is achieved daily, it will be easier to create a cooperative.

Markets

Market organizations are typically state or national bodies that aim to put together consumers and producers. There are a variety of these classes, especially in the herb and flower industry. The downside is that the farmer will not have to make any profits. The downside is that the Commission pays the bulk of such classes. To find these classes, begin by talking to some of the herb and flower organizations and magazines mentioned in the appendix.

Cooperatives

Cooperatives are another way to convince someone else to conduct ads. These are particularly useful for farmers who do not want direct marketing activities or who do not have 'people's skills.' Cooperatives operate by putting together a community of small producers who are all creating the same product(s). They pool their goods to provide the amount needed by the big purchasers. The selling is produced by a co-op salesperson, releasing the farmers for further output time. The downside is that growers do not get the market price for their products (although they can get a slight bonus for quality) and that some of their income may be eaten up by co-op dues (including the wage of the seller). A participant may also be in trouble if the co-op has contracts for an output quantity of X, and its yield is low that year. There might be fees or other punishments, depending on the co-op rules.

There are all sorts of cooperatives in there. A co-op may be as low as eight to ten farmers pooling calves to get a batch of 100 for sale as first-time calves, or it can be a community of farmers working in heirloom deli tomatoes. Co-ops may also be very broad, such as the Dakotas sugar beet cooperatives, where farmers who participate sign tight output contracts.

Carefully research the cooperatives before entering. If you decide to establish one, do your homework first, and talk to a number of other cooperatives. And the loose collectives require laws and regulations for participants to work with. The proportion of revenue to co-op salespeople and ads, how administrative duties should be carried out, and how many farmers will be permitted in the co-op will be decided.

Conclusion

Homesteading is rising in popularity year by year, and it is regarded by many as an attractive and romantic lifestyle. But for all this isn't. Many states allow for varying degrees of homesteading. In the United States, my primary homesteading options are Utah, Western Virginia, Georgia, California, and Missouri. You should be able to provide much of the food in which a small family requires an acre of quality land. Yet it would be difficult to keep it operating at full efficiency and would take a lot of effort.

For pigs or cows, an acre is not enough; it can only accommodate a small flock of chickens, two goats, and a large garden in terms of animals. 5 – 10 acres will be more natural for a truly self-sufficient life. Expect to spend at least $250,000 on building a small home-like, buying a home with sufficient land, machinery, farm planning, etc. In terms of income tax, housing, electricity, equipment (gas, insurance, repairs), animal feed, and more, you'll have an annual expense of around $20,000 a year. If you're able to put the time and hard work into this, it can be a very satisfying way to live.

Homesteading is a way of life and a mentality, and you don't really have to live on a farm to get going. By steadily becoming more self-sufficient and simplifying your life, you will advance slowly step by step towards your ultimate dream of living a homesteader's life.